Embattled Critic

EMBATTLED CRITIC

Views on Modern Art

BY JOHN CANADAY

Farrar, Straus and Company

NEW YORK

For Katherine

FOREWORD:

Author to Reader

Most of the essays collected in this volume were written in the course of duty for *The New York Times*, and hence were produced under circumstances that most people do not think of as applying to a writer. When you work for a newspaper, you do not sit down to invoke the muse at your, or her, leisure. A critic on a newspaper is subject not only to short deadlines but also to the journalistic institution called "the news peg," a current event upon which his essay must hang.

Sometimes this means that an exhibition by an important painter gives you the chance to write a general discussion of his art. Or several exhibitions opening by coincidence during a single week will suggest, in combination, a subject. And occasionally there appears to be nothing to write about yet there is still your space waiting on the page, so you have to find some nominal connection between the calendar and something you have wanted to say for a long time, and you have a chance to say it.

On the whole, the news peg is a rewarding discipline. It forces you to extend your boundaries because it may demand that you look into a subject you would otherwise neglect. But after a few weeks, the topical reference is superfluous to anything the essay manages to say of lasting interest, so I have eliminated the pegs from the majority of the essays here. For instance, the piece on "Children, Amateurs and Artists" was originally pegged to a convention of teachers held in New York City and a display of art-education techniques held at the Museum of Modern Art for the delegates. No reference to these facts remains. On the other hand, difficulties were involved in excising references to the exhibition that occasioned some comments on Miró and Calder, so I have simply let them stand. The reader will recognize that this is true of occasional other pieces.

Frequently I have combined two or three articles, or parts of them, into a single essay for this book. This explains the appearance of more than one date of first publication given at an essay's end, as well as connecting passages that never appeared in *The Times*.

Something else that newspaper readers do not realize is that the articles they read are affected by being tailored to fit a given space. Normally, space is short. I have heard of newspaper men who write short and have to add to fill, but most of us write long and have to cut to fit. I have put some of these cuts back into the essays as they appear here, and I have also changed a word here and there for one that seemed more felicitous. But I have not allowed myself the privilege of second-guessing through rewriting. There are statements in these essays that I would modify in one direction or another if I were making them again for the first time, but it has seemed best to let them ride, with their datelines explaining that any apparent contradictions represent changes of mind. A critic should be allowed to change his mind, and in fact should not be permitted to continue as a critic once he has lost the capacity to do so.

I have been particularly careful not to modify any statements that have brought me under fire. A petition for my discharge from my position on *The Times* was widely circulated by a reputable professor because I stated that brainwashing went on in universities and museums, rather than saying "some" universities and museums. It seems to me that even a professor of art education should have recognized that "some" was implied in context, but since I had originally considered putting in "some" and then had decided not to slow the sentence by this superfluous qualification, I did not change the passage for republication.

In an effort to give this volume some coherence, the essays are grouped under several classifications rather than ordered by date. "Happy New Year" was my first article as art critic for *The Times*. It appeared on Sunday, September 6, 1959, and was also the first of several articles that so offended one group of avant-garde painters and their sympathizers that a letter of objection signed by forty-nine of them was presented to the paper. It was published on the art page of Sunday, February 26, 1961.

Although this letter caused me distress upon receipt, I have since grown so fond of it that it is reprinted here as an appendix, along with a fair selection from more than 600 letters which it in turn inspired. The selection is based on letters published in *The Times* on the two subsequent Sundays.

I cannot let this book go without admitting that the one brilliant spot in it, where painting as practiced today is compared to the art of fencing, is borrowed. It appears in the second article, "A Blue Note," but it was first tossed off in a letter to me from a friend who is without question the finest critic and art historian at work today. He refused to let me give him proper credit, contending that this kind of borrowing has always been "good humanistic practice." Nevertheless I thank him, although he must remain unidentified.

I would like also to thank The New York Times Company for permission to reprint, as well as the magazine *Horizon*. Articles that originally appeared in *Horizon* are acknowledged individually at their ends.

John Canaday

New York, August, 1961

CONTENTS

LIST OF ILLUSTRATIONS

PART ONE:
Questions and Objections

ARTIST AND CRITIC:
Dangers of the Critical Graph.

A critic should ask himself from time to time whether critics in general, including himself as a member of a band rather than as an individual, are necessary, beneficial, only harmless, or actually harmful forces. There are reasons to regard them as the last—to the extent, at any rate, that they are responsible for a schizoid condition peculiar to avant-garde art in the middle third of the twentieth century.

Modern art's typical symptoms of schizophrenia—delusions of persecution and omnipotence—are complicated by a bad case of narcissism that in its own turn splits in two directions. With one eye cocked on itself as innovational, contemporary art has cocked the other in the opposite direction, toward itself as history, the temporary end result of a long development.

This divided focus is not conducive to clear vision, and its contradiction is summarized in a term conceived in recent years, "museum of modern art." (We are talking about the term, not about any one of the institutions bearing that or similar titles in this or other countries.) It is a term implying a stance with one foot in the grave of the past and the other on the banana peel of the moment.

Thus combining impaired vision with precarious footing, critics have come up with some bizarre rationalizations and have stimulated artists to some curious expressions leading to further bizarre analyses, thence to even more curious artistic expressions, and so on in a circle of intellectual incest. This circle has been winding like an ingrown hair ever since critic-historians began operating on a double standard by which avant-garde art was found interesting to the extent that it was (a) completely original, and (b) the natural consequence of the originality that was immediately contemporary last week. Week by month by year by century by millenium, the origins of modern art have been traced back to the art of the prehistoric caves.

The paradox of rejecting the past with contempt and at the same time calling on it for a certificate of legitimacy seems never to have disturbed the practitioners of that form of critical graph-making that evaluates the present and divines the future by charting the course of the past.

The technique of prophecy by graph has been applied to the stock market and other variable factors of contemporary life, but art is a special case in which developments can be warped into their expected shape by a watchful avant-garde. That is, you can *expect* the market to go up or down because that is what it should logically do to maintain the graph-pattern, but you can't *make* it do so. But you can create works of art that comply with an expected direction—and that is a terrible thing.

Instead of following a natural development induced by a truly profound response to life, art can self-consciously set out to do what is anticipated by those who chart it. Thus innovation ceases to be innovation, and becomes only the next step in a predetermined and hence not very adventurous course. In a day when art is supposed to be adventurous and exciting beyond the art of any other day, it toes the line as much as it has done in its least imaginative periods. The fact that the line resembles a roller-coaster makes it no less devoid of surprise, and the fact that the swoops and rises and descents may make you catch your breath when you are going along for the ride, does not affect the fact that you are in an amusement park, not involved with life itself.

To whatever extent critics are responsible for all this, and I think the extent is great, they are a vicious element—not vicious by intention, but no less vicious in effect for all that. Critics should not know artists and artists should not know critics. But since we can't make a law against such fraternization, a critic's obligation is to make certain that what he writes (and talks) is after-the-fact judgment on what the artist creates. And the artist should create without thinking of the critic or of his, the artist's, position on a graph.

June 25, 1961

A BLUE NOTE:

Melancholy Reflections of Possible Interest to Painters and Fencers.

Since the death of impressionism and the perfection of the camera, painters and estheticians have argued from a deterministic point of view to preclude a contemporary school of realistic imagery interpretatively employed. The vast and wonderful visible world has been discarded as if it had no connection with another vastness, our inner experience.

But determinism can be an easy, after-the-fact dodge. The argument that the visible world is exhausted as material for painting is surely nonsense. We hear that Degas, as the great draftsman of the latter nineteenth century, captured an image of the world with such finality that he put an end to a development that began with Giotto. But Degas might have said that about his idol, Ingres. Ingres could have said it of his, Raphael. Anybody could have said it after the Van Eycks, during the last 500 years. But nobody did, and everybody kept on going. The artist today does carry a heavy burden of comparison with the past, but instead of being too timid to meet it, he might regard it as an inheritance to be cherished and built upon.

The gloomiest implication of the present specialized run-in-a-school-like-so-many-fish approach to the problem of what to paint and how, which has reduced painting to its present desperate condition, is the implication that painting is done for as an independent art. This is just about as unhappy an idea as can be imagined. But it may be true, and it is an idea accepted, if only half-consciously, by many people to whom painting means more than any other art. A critic whose favorite phrase is a reverent "art of our time" may say over a cocktail that it is a lousy time for painting, honestly unaware that what he writes implies consistently that painting has broken its equivalent of the sound barrier and has beat the rest of our civilization by getting its men into space. Or a critic whose favorite plug word for the new painting is "vitality" looks at photographs of the selections for the latest big show and says, "Same old stuff," then goes ahead to write it up with his habitual contention that it is all brand new.

I wonder, on this evidence, whether painting today does not occupy the same position in our life that fencing does. Until the invention of firearms, fencing was necessary in order to defend one's life and honor. But after that it became a pastime for people who liked to do it or to look at it, and the same may be true of painting. It used to be a part of life, but now it is a kind of residual sport. This would explain the appetite for novelty, the search for something new at any cost, the emphasis on fashionable values rather than fundamental human ones and, above all, the attitude, basic to our society, that the artist is an amusing parasite.

Such an idea, that painting is in its dog days, is one that I would reject entirely if I could. To accept it, however, is not treachery to a cause. If our time is one of those that cannot sustain independent painting, we are not going to change the time by trying to change painting.

The next question, in all its flat unanswerableness, is "Where next?" or "What are we going to do?" The fact that the question can arise at all is the most discouraging sign that the great days of painting are running out again, as they did between classical antiquity and, say, Giotto. Of course, there is no going back. Anybody would rather see the race for novelty go on, with its cycle of temporary relief, then staleness, then relief, and so on, than to see artificial respiration applied to a corpse. But, as a beginning, painters might look around them, beyond their studio walls.

If it doesn't work, then that's that. After all, the world will be here as long as there are people to respond to it, and when the time is ripe (deterministically), artists may rediscover nature without trying.

In the meantime, the fencing match is diverting to follow —even when we know that it is only an exercise carried on behind foils and guards.

September 27, 1959

MANNA AND MUTATIONS:
Experiments, Museums, Verbal Acrobats and
the Public.

An extraordinary circumstance of much contemporary art criticism is that its major premise, when contemporary painting is under sympathetic examination, is taken for granted by the critic but not understood by the reader. This premise is far from universally held but it is widely held and, when held, is so fundamental that to state it would be like beginning an article "I am breathing as I write."

The premise is that contemporary experimental painting is built around a void—the absence of those common faiths that until our century demanded expression in painting. When this painter or that painter is extolled in terms that would lead the reader to think of him as a modern Michelangelo, what the critic means, as often as not, is that considering the goallessness of painting, this man is good; that although the contemporary painter has been left with nothing to tell us about except himself and his art, this particular one speaks with more flair, grace or vigor than most.

Once this premise is accepted, the phenomenon of experimental painting becomes important as a point of departure for the exploration of its relationship to the past, with which it need no longer be compared, and to the social and philosophical aspects of the present that make it what it is. In this context there is no such thing as an uninteresting work of art —good or bad—and even an inherently pointless daub may become fascinating just as, for the biologist, mutations in plants or living creatures, induced by X-rays, are interesting even though they are monsters and disasters if compared with the normal organisms from which they are sports.

The painter today uses his studio as a laboratory to produce such mutations because, left out of the Table of Organization of the modern world, he has been forced into a position where he can survive only as a prostitute, a parasite— or a discoverer. His only hope as an honest man is to produce a mutation that will fascinate and breed true, to which his name will be attached as originator and propagator.

But great discoveries come hard and rarely, and the fact that what the painter produces is freakish is not surprising. The chaotic, haphazard and bizarre nature of modern art is easily explained: the painter finally settles for whatever satisfaction may be involved in working not as an independent member of a society that needs him, but as retainer for a small group of people who as a profession or as a hobby are interested in the game of comparing one mutation with another.

Yet, at the back of the artist's mind and the minds of everyone engaged in the performance and observation of these laboratory experiments, there is always the hope that the next mutation will be the one that everyone is waiting for —not just another spectacular novelty, but a new form that will serve the present as effectively as the old forms served the past. That is why such serious consideration is given to so much experimental painting that turns out to be trash.

In the process of selection and evaluation a great deal of trash must be examined carefully before it is discarded. But a sinister factor in contemporary art is that an excess of hopeful tolerance for experimental work simply because it is experimental has brought too much trash into public exhibitions under impressive auspices. Museums exhibiting contemporary art in an effort to summarize the scene at the moment may be creating a lay audience that not only tolerates trash but demands it. Trashy art, whether it is painting, music, literature, or another, may be exciting, and the public's first question about an exhibition is beginning to be not whether the art is good, but whether it is stimulating.

This false emphasis should suggest to such museums the undemocratic question of whether it was a good idea in the first place to bring to the millions something that just might have been better left to the few. The plain fact is that, for good or ill, our exhibition techniques, which have been so successful for three decades in educating a large public to an interest in modern art—without much understanding of it— are apparently transforming the nature of art and its audience.

An exhibition that continues to haunt me because I found it disastrously inclusive of experimental trash yet exciting as a display, was the Museum of Modern Art's 1959 "Sixteen Americans." By the explicit statement of its director, Dorothy C. Miller, the show was made up of "choices not intended as final judgments," but they were accepted as final by an audience not given to reading forewords. Miss Miller "wished to share with the museum's public some of the interest and excitement" (that word) "experienced in exploring American art in 1959," and she did so in a symptomatic exhibition.

The symptoms—large scale, violent effects, strainings after novelty, forcings to the ultimate degree based on the experiments of an earlier avant-garde—indicated that art is being subjected to induced rather than natural mutations to supply mass stimulation at the expense of significant expression. The prestige of the museum suggests that the exhibited work must be significant, but a public avid for understanding yet unable to understand what it sees wants an explanation to hang onto. We come thus to the verbal acrobat who satisfies the need and has made art something to talk about rather than to look at. He has produced the mutation of an art unable to support itself spiritually, an art that dies unless it supplies material for verbalizing.

"Sixteen Americans" supplied a perfect example of this dependence in one of a series of lectures by Leo Steinberg called "Contemporary Art and the Plight of Its Public." In discussing the work of Frank Stella, which is composed of wide black stripes and narrow white ones drawn precisely upon huge canvases, Mr. Steinberg reminded me of a diver in one of those old movies where we used to see the man go off the high platform, hit the water, disappear in a great splash, and then, with the film reversed, emerge from the splash feet first to sail upward in a graceful curve to land securely on the platform once more.

Mr. Steinberg performed this illusion by describing the acute, complicated and esoteric pleasures afforded him by Stella's stripe painting, to the point where I was ready to throw him away (along with Stella), and then by admitting that quite possibly the painting was junk, and that what he saw in it might have nothing whatsoever to do with what the painter had put there. All of this was great sport, although when I told Mr. Steinberg what he had reminded me of, he did not seem to like it very much.

Mr. Steinberg concluded his talk with an analogy between the fall of manna in the desert and contemporary art. From

the tape of his lecture, here is the quote from Exodus, six-
teenth chapter, followed by his comments:

"In the morning the dew lay round about the host. And
when ° ° ° [it] was going up, behold, upon the face of the
wilderness there lay a small round thing, as small as the hoar-
frost on the ground. And when the children of Israel saw it
° ° ° they wist not what it was. And Moses said unto them,
This is the bread which the Lord hath given you to eat.
° ° ° Gather of it every man according to his eating. ° ° °
And the children of Israel did so, and gathered, some more,
some less. And when they did mete it with an omer, he that
gathered much had nothing over, and he that gathered little
had no lack; they gathered every man according to his eating.
° ° ° But some of them left of it until the morning, and it
bred worms and stank. ° ° ° And the house of Israel called
the name thereof Manna ° ° ° and the taste of it was like
wafers made with honey. And Moses said ° ° ° Fill an omer
of it to be kept for your generations; that they may see the
bread wherewith I have fed you in the wilderness. ° ° ° So
Aaron laid it up before the Testimony, to be kept."

"The reason this manna made me think of contemporary
art," Mr. Steinberg continued, "is not only (a) that it was a
Godsend, or (b) that it was a desert food; or (c) that no
one knew exactly what it was ('they wist not what it was');
or (d) that a part of it was immediately put into a museum,
as they say here 'a testimony for the generations'; or (e) that
the taste of it has remained a mystery, for the word here
translated as 'a wafer' is in fact a blind guess; the Hebrew
word at this point is one that occurs nowhere else in ancient
Hebrew literature and one does not know what it means,
whence the legend that the taste of manna was unfixed—it
tasted to every man according to his wish.

"What struck me most as an analogy, however, is this moral lesson that you are to gather it each day for the day's eating only—not to lay it up for tomorrow as an insurance or investment, making each day's gathering an act of faith."

The questions dodged by this otherwise beautifully pat analogy are how blind we can allow our faith to be in this daily gathering of experimental art, to what degree this faith should be instilled into a lay public and (it is now time to emulsify our metaphors) whether we are not mistaking for manna some forced and poisonous mutations that might better have been done away with in the laboratory than brought into a museum and offered as a source of sustenance.

I am wondering how "Sixteen Americans" might look if the museum were forced to rehang it after five years. Pretty stale, no doubt, and possibly embarrassing. But no matter. The catalogue has put on record the disclaimer that the judgment is not intended as final, and in the meanwhile new excitements will come along that look good—or talk good, which is increasingly what counts. And as long as we can keep excited by talking, we can forget that bothersome clause, "it bred worms and stank."

January 31, March 6, and July 24, 1960.

ODD FORMS OF MODERN CRITICISM:
When "Interested Sympathy" Becomes an Obsession, Anything Can Happen.

One American critic who is an enthusiastic proselytizer for the more extreme forms of contemporary art in this country states that the "uniquely necessary qualification" for a critic of modern art is "interested sympathy." That word "uniquely" pushes things a little far; surely there are criteria for the judgment of modern art that are more important than a predisposition in its favor. But, accepting the necessity for interested sympathy, it seems to me that the real problem in criticism is to recognize the point at which interested sympathy becomes dangerous.

At what level does interested sympathy become partisanship? At what level does partisanship become obsessive proselytism? And at what intensity does this obsession result in such self-delusion that a critic may write honestly about contemporary painting yet from a point of view so warped that rational evaluation becomes impossible?

When sympathy for avant-garde art per se is the assumption behind a critical attitude, criticism can cease to be judgment and become a form of pedantry in which the goal is to find excitement and meaning in an object where they may not exist. Once thus self-deluded, the critic may write perceptively yet from an absurd position. This explains the success of such old gags as the drawing board cover smeared with pen wipings that wins a prize in a serious exhibition.

As an exercise in critical gymnastics on the "Interested Sympathy" premise, let us take a blot of pigment which is before me as I write. It occupies about three inches of a piece of spongy, battered wallboard that served as an easel in an elementary painting class. The blot is a dried and cracked puddle of blue poster paint from which a small bit has run down like a tail; a smaller and similar splatter is off to one side below it. The only art involved in this painting is whatever art was involved in framing it off from the surrounding mess. Yet in writing about it as if it were a painting seriously presented at large scale, one might say something like this:

"Anyone who objects to abstract art on the basis of its 'ivory-towerism' should visit the one-man show of paintings by the new Spanish artist, Ninguno Denada, that opened yesterday at the Node Gallery. In this exhibition, to which the artist gives the over-all title 'The Authority of the Accidental,' the very basis of art as social statement in our time is established once and for all.

"Denada believes that action painting has run its course not only esthetically but also as a product of its social environment, and that the artist is now faced with the obligation to explore the dynamics of inaction.

"As an example, take the powerful composition entitled 'Blue Element.' It might, if reduced to the size of a few inches, look like nothing more than a blot of pigment. Yet at its monumental scale, nearly 10 feet tall, played against a tensional background created by one formal echo of the main mass (lower left) and a heavily textured surface, 'Blue Element' is deeply impressive, a profound expression of our century of crisis, and a disturbing one that should shock us into an awareness of the time in which we live.

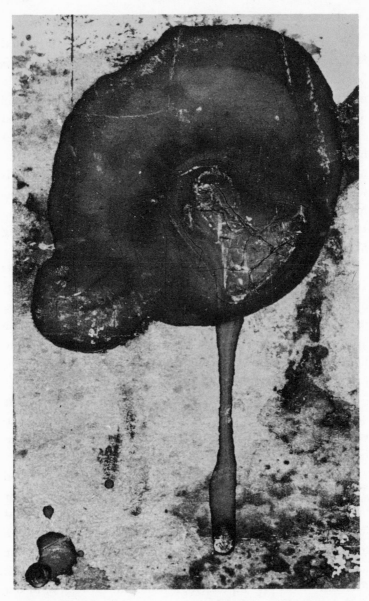

"NINGUNO DENADA": *"BLUE ELEMENT."* Pseudo-painting. Height about 3". Poster color on wallboard.

"How does Denada achieve this? In this way: The huge central element, generally globular in shape, is the very apotheosis of the inertness of matter, while the small, stem-like trail that runs beneath it is abruptly terminated as if an attempted escape from the limitations of material things has been thwarted. This, of course, makes Denada philosophically a pessimist. Yet his feeling that we are trapped in a material world in which spiritual values have been forgotten could hardly have been more forcefully, or more honestly, expressed.

"Like it or not, Denada is an artist of our time, and a courageous one. The future—if we may hazard a prophecy—will recognize in his art the consummate expression of a century in which humankind, having lost its way, created in the work of at least one painter an ultimate expression of the element of courage that is inherent in the recognition of defeat. It is thus that art serves society and history."

Although this is satire it is not burlesque, and even as satire it is not much different from the brainwashing that goes on in universities and museums except that it includes a minimum of jargon. It is not offered here as a gag. In writing it, and perhaps in reading it, one can almost believe in it, and that is the sinister factor in an exercise that otherwise would be farcical.

It is also possible to interpret this blot-art historically within the continuum of valid works, in some such manner as this:

"Denada is at once a revolutionary and the climax of several contemporary movements—their harmonious combination, in fact, and their fulfillment, rather than their rejector. One thinks immediately of his countrymen, Modest Cuixart, whose circular concretions of pigment are reflected in the heavily laden central mass of 'Blue Element,' and Antoni Tapiès, the cavelike textures of whose matter-painting are frankly the source of the rough field against which this element is played.

"But where Cuixart is primarily ornamental, and where Tapiès seems to be groping for some kind of magical hieroglyphical vocabulary, Denada disciplines and thus transforms these borrowed factors as an artist whose first reference is to social rather than to esthetic philosophy or to necromancy.

"Obviously, Denada's biomorphic suggestions hint in the main mass at Miró. But in place of Miró's witty vivacity, Denada employs an almost ponderous weightiness, of such power that where one's first reaction in front of a Miró is delight, one responds to Denada with an abrupt realization that one's concept of the world is being challenged, and that an answer is being offered.

"It is thus that men must have felt when, six and a half centuries ago, they first stood before Giotto's frescoes in the Arena Chapel and were faced with the transformation of art from a familiar and threadbare formula into a revelation of the nature of a world they inhabited yet had not understood.

"Admittedly, Denada is still, at this stage of his development, a little awkward. But so was Giotto, who also developed from painters preceding him yet transfigured our vision of the world by fulfilling the tentative formal revolution of Cimabue."

This kind of pseudo-analysis could go on and on, bringing us to the artist's title of his show, "The Authority of the Accidental," which he might be asked to explain in his own words:

"By the authority of the accidental, I mean to harmonize

the elements of chance and self-determination that combine to cast the courses of our lives. Man has acted on the premise that he can exercise control over his environment. But we have gone far enough now to discover that for all our development of science, of government, of self-knowledge, we are still subject first of all to the force of hazard. Therefore, instead of beginning a painting with the assumption of order I begin it with the assumption of hazard. My inspiration is drawn from the most irrelevant and accidental aspects of the visual world—not plants, human beings and so on, whose growth follows a pattern, but such things as blots, rips and fragments of this and that, where the element of hazard predominates.

"Yet even in blots, what I call the 'laws of inaction' determine the nature of action. The action of a bit of paint that drips from the brush without your intention forms an 'accidental' shape, yet this shape is determined by the weight, texture and velocity of the drip. I, therefore, begin with forms that appear accidental and, while attempting to retain the quality of accident, invest it with a kind of order that accepts the authority of accident as the source of our lives, yet indicates that we may survive by adjusting ourselves to that authority."

Enough. There is not a painter or a philosophy to which the pseudo-painting "Blue Element" could not be related in this fashion, once the assumption of its legitimacy is accepted. That is why the premise of "sympathetic interest" (a crutch, by the way, that is required only by contemporary avant-garde art), must be more cautiously examined than it usually is, if criticism of contemporary painting is to mean anything. Furthermore, the distinction between one painting and another must be more than the distinction between "the really novel and the falsely novel," as another proselytizer states the problem. No: the distinction must be between the merely novel and the truly meaningful.

October 23, 1960

TENTH STREET:
A Report Without Recommendation for Mercy.

The Tenth Street idea, which took root in the early years of the last decade and still flourishes, is simple and admirable: to provide galleries in a low rent area where artists who might otherwise be unable to do so may show their work to anyone sufficiently interested to come to a sordid part of the city to look at it. The area is improving today but Bowery bums still filter into it, quarreling and panhandling.

The Tenth Street galleries are between Third and Fourth Avenues for the most part, with sprouts as far off as Twelfth Street and a new shoot, practically in suburbia, on Great Jones Street. Typically they are small, close, low-ceilinged compartments in bad to moderately good repair. In raw weather, like last week's, their whitewashed do-it-yourself interiors (lots of wallboard, most of it needing a few more nails) have a nice coziness with their gas heaters.

The majority are cooperative ventures, and even the privately managed ones maintain an air of benevolence toward artists and informality toward the visitor that distinguishes them from the sleek or plushy décor and the flinty commercialism of their uptown counterparts, where, of course, the downtown artist hopes eventually to come to harbor.

What happens when the critic goes down to Tenth Street? Agreeably, the atmosphere is not beatnik, but sensible and serious. At several of the galleries attractive young women with well-washed hair are in attendance, and the stigmata of the Philistine—a haircut, necktie and shined shoes—are apparent on an occasional male.

But already these introductory comments indicate what is wrong with the relationship of the critic to Tenth Street. He enters a special environment, where local color makes up for inconvenience, and critical judgment is relaxed as a gesture to the special function of the galleries as clearing houses for talents to be judged by sub-professional standards.

This is all wrong. My contention is that Tenth Street is the last place in town where critical judgment should be softened. Too many people paint, too many fourth-rate painters are treated with respect, too many second-rate ones with reverence and too many first-rate ones are deified as if they had genius instead of talent and ideas. The assumption that young painters should be encouraged is absurd and in the end vicious. No one owes them a debt of gratitude for their adoption of a dubious profession; they should be cut down in battalions, on the principle of weeding and pruning, to allow the ones with vigor to rise again.

The critic should have no concern with the artist's problems. His job is to look at things as objectively as possible in a field where all values but his own may be subjective—not an easy job but one easily abused. Courtesy is not his function, although it is his constant temptation. He cannot expect to be loved. When he rejects a young painter on the occasion of a first one-man show, he may break a heart at worst or infuriate the painter and his well-wishers at best. And the critic must suffer from the knowledge that although he is as honest as he knows how to be, he can be wrong.

All of this is preparatory to a considered statement, which is that on my Tenth Street tour during a presumably typical week of openings I saw nothing that would be much missed if obliterated, very little that I could imagine giving satisfaction even to the artists themselves, and plenty that was plain bad. To be merciless, at the Brata Gallery, John Krushenick's drawings seemed to me devoid of taste, talent or ideas, and his companion exhibitor, William Creston, working in scrubs of black ink, managed to be totally inept in a field where to be inept at all is next to impossible.

On the other hand, Emily Mason at the Area Gallery exhibited some really lovely pastels (the adjective has been examined, and it stands) that were selling well. She also exhibited more ambitious oils in which she was out of her depth.

Between these extremes, other galleries exhibited assorted exercises. The Camino Gallery had a good idea for a group show. "In view of the predominance of strong color contrasts in contemporary art," the announcement said, "this exhibition attempts to focus attention on works with close color ranges. Concentrated participation is demanded from the viewer for the recognition of the subtleties explored in this selection." But I found the demands greater than the rewards, although I went back a second day to concentrate further.

At the Tanager Gallery, founded as long ago as 1952 and now as smart and prosperous looking as an uptown place, some unnecessary collages were exhibited by John Grillo, an alumnus of reputation. At the new Great Jones Gallery, a

Tenth Street with galleries, New York City, January, 1960. Photograph by Neal Boenzi, *The New York Times.*

basement entered by a ramp and attractively adapted, I found Ian Pinkerson's paintings a repetitious collection of desolate, badly painted heads in ill-composed space. I was sorry about this, because two nice youngsters whom I suspected of being the gallery's owner and the pictures' painter deserve better of their venture—by humanitarian standards but not by critical ones.

Nor am I able to be much kinder to Robert La Hotan, who, at the James Gallery, exhibits a large number of routine canvases of the Hans Hofmann persuasion in which the artist disembowels himself in public, a practice I deplore when it is not done with consummate aplomb. Other galleries offered work in one familiar but undigested manner after another.

Actually, none of this should be unexpected, and in the end that is the real difficulty down Tenth Street way. It is not a place where new ideas are offered for consideration, but one where the clichés of the uptown galleries are repeated at a less satisfactory level. Obviously, one can't find a new idea per week; one trouble with contemporary art is precisely that fifty years of innovations have so whetted our appetites that we expect new excitements to develop more rapidly than they legitimately can.

Hence, Tenth Street's dilemma is that on one hand it can reflect the current scene only as second-string to the galleries uptown, while, on the other, no matter how assiduously it may forage, it cannot find sufficient nourishment to sustain itself in the function of discoverer.

Meantime, the important thing to remember about Tenth Street is that it must not be coddled simply because it exists. This means malice toward none, but not charity toward any, for charity in this case is debilitating to the recipient. It also means bad mail on the critic's desk in the morning.

But as a postscript, let us add that Tenth Street's sincerity, even in those cases where it is juvenile and misdirected, is refreshing after the high-pressure techniques elsewhere, and that the ratio between Tenth Street sales at modest prices and those of certain uptown painters at tremendous ones is frequently out of kilter. The artificially induced hubbub that makes a major reputation out of a mediocre artist must be painful beyond imagination to the identically mediocre artist who remains unknown and unsold. If the critic's lot is not a happy one, the painter's is worse.

January 17, 1960

NEW YORK, U.S.A.:
The City and "The New York School."

An obligation to perform an errand took me the other day from Times Square to City College, and the trip in turn inspired some unexpected reflections upon the physical spectacle of New York City as a stimulant to a dominant school of contemporary American painting, as well as upon the spiritual limitations this school has in turn imposed.

Approaching the campus of City College along 133d Street you pass what I am certain I cannot be sued for calling a slum. The sidewalks were littered with cancerous discarded furniture; the houses were abominable and picturesque in their decay; upon their steps, men and women laughed and quarreled and children whined for ice cream. There were some drunks. Where a house had been wrenched out of the row, more children played on the scab, with a three-sided refrigerator and a rusty kitchen stove, along with other decomposing remnants of matter, as toys. (They seemed happy enough; it was a beautiful sunny, windy day.)

This was one side of the street. On the other, tower after tower after tower of the Manhattanville housing project rose, the windows still crossed with white X's and all the mess and confusion of construction still surrounding them.

Where the street ends in Convent Avenue and the campus of City College, you look uptown at the curve of a pure Greek amphitheatre blocked by an unsightly many-storied wall of concrete—Lewisohn Stadium and its entrance. Beyond that, on the other side of the street, a huge building is in costume for a medieval ball, all Gothic filigrees, buttresses and spires.

Inside the campus gates, in the bookstore where I asked for information, paperbacks on every subject in the world were lined up along with phonograph records which must have been a summary of all music, and a definitive selection of candy bars, the chief source of nourishment in this general quarter, to judge from this counter and a couple of dozen others in small stores everywhere around and from the wrappers on the pavements and sidewalks. Any remaining counterspace in the bookstore was jammed with odds and ends of things costing 15 cents to a dollar and designed to complicate or simplify life.

On the campus, boys and girls and men and women of every race, creed, color and shape except American Indian were dressed in everything except war bonnets, from pure Ivy League uniforms to dungarees and T-shirts, from saris to Bermuda shorts. It was lunch time and everyone was going somewhere else, fast.

Outside again, errand completed and en route to the subway via Convent Avenue, I had to buck large numbers of unathletic looking young men in gym shorts, apparently just released from compulsory activities on the playing field and mixing with the traffic on their way back to the lockers. From there to the subway it was a matter of everything—laundromats, groceries, branch banks, small shops of every kind, whatever you want to mention. There was even a small park in a triangle left by one of Broadway's intersections with right-angled streets, as verdant as anything in Paris and lined with benches occupied by some clean and motionless old gentlemen alongside some disorderly types, male and female, who will enjoy whatever kind of immortality is afforded by the police blotter.

This turbulent and noisy and routine and even banal spectacle offered, in every fractional part, what used to be called "material for the artist." But I wondered what in the world an artist could do with it today. Tiny bit by tiny bit it was inexhaustible but its variety was defeating. The latter nineteenth-century painters who left something like a comprehensive record of their Paris and its spirit could not have begun to record and interpret this limited area. It could yield a thousand paintings to the picturesque realist, even the poetic realist, and certainly the socially-conscious realist, but these would be without a common denominator beyond their incidental geographical one.

But the area has a common denominator, which is a kind of boiling energy that extends through the entire city. Park Avenue and Third Avenue in process of spectacular and elegant rebuilding share that denominator, and so does the rest of the island in its physical and emotional flux.

The energetic confusion and the high emotional color of this city explain why the painters called—so appropriately in this light—"The New York School" are obsessed with the sweeping, splashing, lunging, agitated forms typical of the majority of them. It explains too why this style as adopted wholesale all over the country has such a hollow ring in the work of imitators who inhabit the prairies west, the bayous south, and the green hills north, of Manhattan. It explains why contemporary American painting fascinates artists on the other side of the Atlantic, yet repels them even while they adopt it—the cocktail in the country of subtle wines.

It explains in our country the difference between Mark Tobey and Jackson Pollock (a philosopher and an athlete) and it explains why the rigidly controlled school of abstract painting runs such a poor second to action painting on Manhattan Island, and why even Mondrian, in his last years here, began to paint jumpy compositions.

In the ebullience, the vitality, and the exuberance of its first youth the art of abstract expressionism captured the common denominator of a city. But it did not begin to capture the common denominator of a nation; it is New York painting, not American painting. And even as New York painting, there is plenty of question as to whether it gives any order or meaning, as art should do, to the energy it expresses, or whether it has created only explosive fragments. That is my quarrel with even the best of it.

Perhaps abstract expressionism cannot mean anything because the vast welter of New York is in itself meaningless, an unhappy possibility. If so, then the quarrel is not with the artist's limitation but with our time and our city, of which abstract expressionism offers a complete and authentic expression. But it seems to me that the expression is no more complete and authentic than are fireworks as an expression of what the Fourth of July means.

Fireworks are wonderful to look at but I do not think that they offer a very profound experience, and I would not want the sky filled with them all night, year after year. Similarly I enjoy looking at abstract expressionist painting, but there is a limit to how much of it one can take, and I am tired of hearing that its skyrockets are cosmic manifestations.

New York is always called an exciting city, and so it is.

But the things that make it exciting also make it monotonous if they are not tied to something deeper than surface movement and color. That is what I look for in abstract expressionist painting and do not find, and that is why I find it monotonous. A fine place for a visit, but I wouldn't want to live there without the sustenance of those inner human values that are universal—even to New Yorkers—yet are non-existent in the painting of the New York School.

May 22, 1960

HAPPY NEW YEAR:
Thoughts on Critics and Certain Painters as the Season Opens.

The New Year in these parts has so little to do with the first day of January and so much to do with the first Monday in September that Labor Day's Eve, which is tonight, would be a good time to ring the bells and blow the whistles while everyone wishes everyone else the best of everything for the next twelve months—including a lot less pother about abstract expressionism. With any luck, 1959-60 might even go down in history as the year abstract art in general accepted the responsibilities of middle age.

Kandinsky painted the first completely abstract composition half a century ago (forty-nine years, to split hairs), yet we are still talking about "the new art." Impressionism, a genuine scandal where abstract expressionism is a synthetic

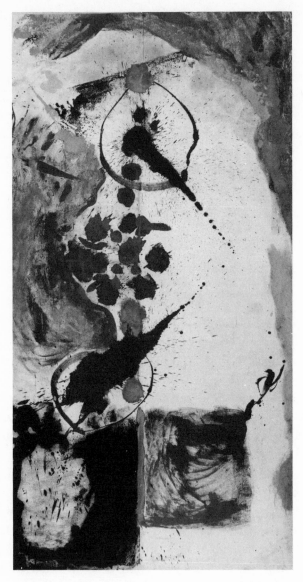

HELEN FRANKENTHALER: *LABOR DAY 1959.* 80¼"
x 42". Oil on canvas. Courtesy André Emmerich
Gallery, New York.

one, took less than half that many years to be born, to mature and to give way in its turn to the various innovations of post-impressionism. And a little quick arithmetic based on the birth and death dates of fauvism, cubism and surrealism as proselytizing movements should make the abstract expressionists feel embarrassed in their protracted adolescence. Fifty years is a long time to have remained so starry eyed, and some of the sparkle, examined at close range, is beginning to look distressingly like crow's feet.

There can be no objection to abstract expressionism as one manifestation of this complicated time of ours. The best abstract expressionists are as good as ever they were—a statement not meant to carry a concealed edge. But as for the freaks, the charlatans and the misled who surround this handful of serious and talented artists, let us admit at least that the nature of abstract expressionism allows exceptional tolerance for incompetence and deception.

The art of the French Salon, recognized as deadly, is the only school comparable in prolix mediocrity to the rank and file of abstract expressionist work today. Yet Salon art did require of its practitioners at least a manual talent for the imitation of academic disciplines, while anyone, literally, can paint in a kind of abstract expressionist idiom. Sweet innocence of technical fetters may even give the most unconsidered daub an individual character. Witness the highly personal work of Betsy the Ape, conspicuous not long ago in the newspapers, but the recipient of the silent treatment in the art magazines. Of course Betsy's work was not art, but it was certainly abstract and, in its own way, quite expressive of her own gay, outgoing self.

Yet the fact that a reasonable, if reprehensible, approximation of abstract expressionism can be executed in ten min-

utes by a novice with a large brush, is not sufficient explanation for so prolific a growth among painters who regard
themselves as professionals. The question is why so many
painters have adopted a form of art that should seem pointless except to the recondite, and why a large public is so
humble in the face of an art that violates every one of its
esthetic convictions. Bad painters we must always have, but
how does it happen that we have them in such profusion in
such a limited field, and why are we taking them so seriously?

The fault, I am afraid, lies quite directly with professors,
museum men and critics, including this writer, who has func-
tioned in all three capacities. In our missionary fervor for
the best of it, we have managed to create the impression that
all abstract art per se must be given the breaks on the probability that there is more there than meets the eye, while all
other art per se must be regarded with suspicion on the
probability that it isn't as good as it looks. Things have come
to the point where it is amusing to dismiss the Renaissance
with a quip, but dangerous to one's critical reputation not
to discover in any second-rate abstract exercise some cosmic
implication.

Ever since poor Ruskin ruined himself by accusing Whistler of throwing a pot of paint in the public's face and losing
the libel suit that Whistler clapped on him, timid critics have
been wiping the paint out of their eyes with a smile. But
critics who think of themselves as adventurous have been
even more responsible for an attitude that has changed art
criticism from a rational evaluative process to a blind defense of any departure from convention, including pretentious novelties.

We suffer, actually, from a kind of mass guilt complex.
Because Delacroix was spurned by the Academy until he

was old and sick, because Courbet had to build his own exhibition hall in 1855 to get a showing for pictures that are now in the Louvre, because Manet was laughed at, because Cézanne worked in obscurity, because Van Gogh sold only one picture during his lifetime, because Gauguin died in poverty and alone, because nineteenth-century critics and teachers and art officials seemed determined to annihilate every painter of genius—because of all this we have tried to atone to a current generation of pretenders to martyrdom. Somewhere at the basis of their thinking, and the thinking of several generations of college students who have taken the art appreciation course, is the premise that wild unintelligibility alone places a contemporary artist in line with great men who were misunderstood by their contemporaries.

Recognizing a Frankenstein's monster when they see it—and lately they can't miss it—some critics and teachers wail, "But what are we going to do? We can't go back to all those old Grant Woods again." Of course it is not a matter of going backward, but forward—somewhere. That we will go forward from abstract expressionism seems unlikely, since it is more and more evident that these artists have either reached the end of a blind alley or painted themselves into a corner. In either case, they are milling around in a very small area—which, come to think of it, may explain why they are increasingly under a compulsion to paint such very large canvases.

In the meanwhile, critics and educators have been hoist with their own petard, sold down the river. We have been had. In the most wonderful and terrible time of history, the abstract expressionists have responded with the narrowest and most lopsided art on record. Never before have painters found so little in so much.

September 6, 1959

NO HAPPY NEW YEAR?
Two Readers Reject a Friendly Greeting.

On the tenth day of May, 1944, on the drill field of the Marine Corps Base at Quantico, Va., as the only dissenting member of a company of recruits that had received the command "column left," this writer executed a brisk right turn. When the clatter of falling musketry had subsided and the column had been put back into order, the drill sergeant, name of Kearley, gave me a piece of his mind. During the fifteen years that have elapsed since the incident, I have felt secure in the knowledge that I had been called everything.

But things changed with the publication in these pages, two weeks ago, of reservations I hold on the score of abstract expressionism. Of the hundred-odd responses to the article, only two were disapproving, yet these two demonstrated that Sergeant Kearley's catalogue of invective was not, after all, definitive. It remained for Daniel Catton Rich, formerly director of the Art Institute of Chicago and presently director of the Worcester Art Museum, to deliver the really wounding word. In a letter dated Sept. 8 he finds me "uninteresting." Even Sergeant Kearley, in spite of our disagreement, found me fascinating in my own way.

Mr. Rich wrote, interestingly, to "The Editor of the Art Page," objecting to the article "Happy New Year—Thoughts on Critics and Certain Painters as the Season Opens":

Dear Sir:

I found John Canaday's article in The New York Times for Sunday, Sept. 6, uninteresting—but irritating. Uninteresting because it includes all the old clichés about abstract expressionism. Irritating in two ways:

First. Canaday assumes that abstract expressionism has reached a dead end and nothing can come of it. How does he know?

To me this is just the old academic approach to any living movement. The "museum man, the professor and the critic" makes the mistake of treating contemporary art as though it were already embalmed art history. And what of the emerging image in abstract expressionism?

Second. Canaday, like a number of the critics who "wail" at what is going on, seems too lazy to discriminate between what is positive and what is grossly imitative. It takes time, it takes sensitivity and it takes insight to project into the idiom of the strictly contemporary. But it can be done.

I recommend to the reader (it won't do Canaday any good) Dr. Jung's incisive remarks on abstract expressionism in his fascinating new book, "Flying Saucers" (Harcourt Brace, 1959).

Sincerely,

DANIEL CATTON RICH.

Mr. Rich asks, "How does he know (that abstract expressionism has reached a dead end)?" I know this by deduction from observation, the same means that bring Mr. Rich to the opposite position. My crystal ball may be no clearer than his, but neither may his be any clearer than mine.

He asks further, "And what of the emerging image in ab-

stract expressionism?" Any emerging image in a school of
painting that has denied the validity of imagery is an admission of defeat, a retrogression rather than an advance, a back-
ing out of the blind alley, and the end of the school's development.

Differences of opinion may be held in friendly opposition.
But when I write an attack aimed quite directly at "the
freaks, the charlatans and the misled who surround a handful of serious and talented men," I do object to being read
from a point of view so entrenched that a man of Mr. Rich's
eminence can find me "too lazy to discriminate between
what is positive and what is grossly imitative."

Finally, Mr. Rich says that it takes time, sensitivity and
insight to project into the idiom of the strictly contemporary.
I know it does. I think that I did so years ago with everybody
else, that I traveled along and that in recognizing the sterility
of a once fertile idiom I am still under way. If I am right,
this could make me more strictly contemporary than Mr.
Rich, leaving him "embalmed" as a distinguished spokesman
for the "new Salon" referred to in my article.

The other letter of objection came from Donald M. Blinken, a collector and art patron who was filled with "dismay
bordering on disbelief" as he read my "moth-eaten clichés."
He suspects that I "would have some difficulty distinguish-
ing a Kline from a De Kooning or a Giacometti from a
Richier," and would "surely" be unable to tell "which Guston
or Rothko or Dickinson was painted ten years ago—which
this year."

Curious, but the names in Mr. Blinken's list (not all
abstract expressionists, by the way) are those of artists whose
work I respect and enjoy, even in the cases where I think

their premises are dubious. In the case of Guston, since many people have asked, I am willing to plump for him as the finest artist of the school. I have followed Guston's work with particular sympathy both before and especially after an hour's talk with him in his studio in St. Louis in 1946, a crucial period in his development.

Mr. Rich and Mr. Blinken, as ardent believers, should welcome an effort to show how a situation built on fraud at worst and gullibility at best has produced a school of such "prolix mediocrity" (my words) that the "grossly imitative" (Mr. Rich's) drives out the good through the action of (you should pardon the cliché) Gresham's Law.

September 20, 1959

IN THE GLOAMING:
Twilight Seems to Be Settling Rapidly for Abstract Expressionism

While there is still time—that is, before its sun sets entirely— we might speak a few last words on the subject of abstract expressionism, since the week's mail has brought with it the latest copy of *It Is*.

It Is is a well-printed periodical that defines itself as "A Magazine for Abstract Art. No Representational Art. No Journalism. Not Surreal." Normally it devotes the bulk of its space to the reproduction and discussion of that form of abstract art classifiable as expressionist. This is natural, since for a decade the bulk of abstract art in America has followed that course of least resistance and quickest profit.

Essentially, *It Is* is a publication of The Club, a free discussion group with quarters downtown where surely more words have been spent, and more coined, on the subject of art than in any other single chamber. The Club rises like a pustule, according to its detractors, or like Olympus, according to its devotees, in that section of New York where abstract art is lived, breathed and almost literally eaten.

As Olympians, the denizens of The Club recognize Jackson Pollock as their Cronus and Willem de Kooning as their Zeus. On the slopes we might find Grace Hartigan, Helen Frankenthaler and Joan Mitchell as the goddesses who compete for the golden apple—Aphrodite, Athene and Hera, although not necessarily respectively. The great legend maker who serves the gods as middleman for mortals is the critic Thomas B. Hess, and his lyre is the magazine *Art News*, of which he is executive editor.

Either the current (and fifth) issue of *It Is* is more sober than its predecessors or this journalist has savvied up considerably so that its contents do not seem to be the pure esoteric balderdash that made the first issues treasures of their kind. There is still plenty that must seem balderdash to those of us who perceive Olympus but dimly and from afar, yet most of the sentences now parse and the majority of the words used are to be found in Webster's. This in spite of the fact that the magazine's concluding article, an attack by P. G. Pavia on the critic Hilton Kramer, editor of the magazine *Arts*, is, as nearly as I can figure out between the lines of the eccentric typography, an objection to the fact that Mr. Kramer writes English pretty well.

Elsewhere, *It Is*'s concessions to maturity are possibly the result of a body blow delivered by Alfred H. Barr Jr., who as everyone knows is director of the museum collections at the Museum of Modern Art and without any question at all the most powerful tastemaker in American art today, and probably in the world.* This summer in *Esquire*—we are in the presence of history here, for never before have *Esquire* and *It Is* been mentioned in the same breath—this summer in *Esquire,* Mr. Barr was quoted as follows:

"During the past dozen years we have had a strong movement: Abstract-expressionism, which has enjoyed an international reputation and great success here. The vigor and quality of this movement is bound to generate a reaction—but where we are going to go I'm not willing to prophesy. What I see is a new concern with figure, and a movement toward a new severe style."

Mr. Barr's statement is of course in no way derogatory to abstract expressionism and is not phrased as an obituary, but an obituary it is, and no less so for being, like more obvious obituaries, a pat on the back for the corpse. There is not a dealer in town, nor a collector, nor yet a painter hoping to hang in the Museum of Modern Art who doesn't study each of Mr. Barr's syllables in an effort to deduce what he should offer for sale, what he should buy, or what he should paint. If Mr. Barr sees "a new concern with figure, and a movement toward a new severe style," there is going to be a vast weeding out in the gallery lists this fall, a vast indifference on the part of buyers to what they fought to get hold of last year and a rush toward the art stores where those little books called "How to Draw" are for sale.

* In a letter to *The New York Times,* Mr. Barr rejected the title of tastemaker and made other objections to this article. His letter appeared on *The New York Times* art page of September 25, 1960.

Meanwhile, *It Is* reports seven panels on the "Hess-Problem," the nature of which is not clear although it is much concerned with abstract expressionism as an "unwanted title." Attention is given to whether the term should be "abstract Expressionism" with a small a and a capital E, or "abstract-Expressionism," same a and E plus a hyphen, or "Abstract Expressionism," capital A and capital E but no hyphen. Apparently some panel members refused to talk unless the term was capitalized, uncapitalized, hyphenated, or dehyphenated according to their wishes.

In the panel's fifth session this technical point had become so important that the subject was changed to "The Structural Concept of the Twentieth Century"—"in the hope," according to Mr. Pavia, who reported the session, "that 'structural' would balance the word 'abstract' and solve the problem." Mr. Pavia further said that a compact paraphrase of the complaints would be "a bastard word, a bastard idea and a bastard artist," a resounding summary, which, out of context, gives an entirely false impression that the gap between what the artists think and what the public has thought for a long time has at last been closed.

It Is also includes a transcript from the tape of the panel held last March at the Philadelphia Museum School of Art, with Philip Guston, Robert Motherwell, Ad Reinhardt, Harold Rosenberg and Jack Tworkov as participants, a panel reported on this page the next Sunday, April 3, to the satisfaction of nobody much. The speakers have revised the tape for publication in *It Is,* which does not seem quite fair, but it is still full of nuggets of the rich, raw and irrational quality that marked the improvisational struggles of that session.

The people who write in *It Is* are great ones for rejoinders and double rejoinders. Hans Hofmann having said certain things in an article, "Space and Pictorial Life," William H. Littlefield objects. Mr. Hofmann answers back. Barbara Butler (in the best-written piece to appear in *It Is* to date, unless that distinction belongs to David Hare with his "Talk on Sculpture," which is not quite journalism but is nevertheless intelligible) attacks Kenneth Tynan, the drama critic, because he does not believe in abstract painting. She asks, "How silly can one get?"

This is the question most people will ask after thumbing through *It Is*, even in its present moderately chastened state. But the question is not pertinent. The pertinent question is how a group of serious and not-stupid artists (forget the hangers-on) year after year have been able to concentrate their attention on works of art like 90 per cent of the ones illustrated here, from Milton Resnick's front cover to Paul Jenkins' tailpiece. The "vigor and quality" of abstract expressionism referred to by Mr. Barr must indeed have been great to have sustained for so long so much repetitious painting.

But the sustenance now seems exhausted. Art feeds on life, and for that reason abstract expressionism, never having learned to feed upon anything except its own vitals, is now left in a pretty pass—no vitals and no fodder. Hence the current *It Is* has a quality no longer avant-garde but retrospective. In the twilight of abstract expressionism, let all this be a warning to the next avant-garde to avoid suicide by auto-cannibalism.

September 11, 1960

CHILDREN, AMATEURS, AND ARTISTS:
The Artist's First Job, Everything Considered,
Is to Grow Up.

The word "art" has a new meaning, and there is no word
now for the wonderful thing that art used to be. Children
do art. Mother in her middle age takes up art. So does
grandma. Even great grandma. The results are usually dis-
missable even by close relatives, but they are often extraordinary, sometimes fascinating, and even, in extreme exceptions,
something like art, and this is where a dangerous confusion
of values sets in.

Many painters who think of themselves as artists and who
are accepted as professionals, would do well to compare
their work with that of children and amateurs and ask themselves just how far, as mature or maturing artists, they have
gone beyond the elementary stages of "the art experience,"
a deadly phrase dear to those who teach youngsters and
hobbyists. They might discover that they are doing nothing
more than applying with a high degree of manual dexterity,
but no maturity of conception or purpose, artistic devices
suitable to the elementary classroom.

The question comes down to what you mean by art. I do
not like the use of the word in "art education" but there is
no other word for the kind of expressive release, through
materials also used by the artist, that this kind of "art" gives
to children or amateurs. Call it "the color experience" or "the
tactile experience" or several other experiences; it does not

really add up to "the art experience." What is called the art experience is fine for children, and as adults they will be readier to go beyond it for having had it. But it should not be confused with art. Yet it has become thus confused, and, which is really bad, *art* has become confused with *it*.

One of the most attractive paintings I know, outside the realm of legitimate art, one that hangs on my own wall and gives me constant pleasure, is the work of an 82-year-old illiterate Negro woman, a onetime field hand from Mississippi, who in a Philadelphia settlement house was given paints and brushes for the first time in her life. Fascinated to discover that a straight line topped by a fuzzy circle looked like a tree, and limiting herself to her two favorite colors—pink and orange—she produced, on a piece of soft gray paper that came to hand, a landscape that continues to delight me after five years of daily familiarity.

But in the long run, all things considered, Leonardo da Vinci was a greater artist than this old woman, whose name I have forgotten. And if by some nightmare circumstance I had to destroy my pink and orange landscape or agree to having the Louvre's "Mona Lisa" hacked to bits, I would tear up a picture that gives me pleasure in order to save one of which I am sick and tired.

But I would not destroy my landscape to save any one of a great many contemporary paintings now on sale at prices from $100 to $10,000 in New York galleries, or many of the same breed in certain museums and certain important collections, because these paintings, too, are essentially the work of amateurs or of children who have developed technical skill. Furthermore, they are paintings whose pretension has robbed them of the freshness and expressiveness that alone, and in rare cases, make amateur painting come close to art.

Art is not a visceral release but a refinement or intensification of the human spirit through a combination of emotional impulse and intellectual discipline. The peculiarity of contemporary painting is that the line between the artist and the amateur has been lost. The "art" education of children is not responsible for this loss; the responsibility lies further along the line, at the point where mere flair is confused with disciplined growth, when it is really only a continuation of infantile or juvenile release.

A student is even lucky in many schools if technique is supposed to go far beyond the amateur level. Many a college tries not to "kill" the student's still childish response to the pure kinetic pleasure of playing with materials, and many a studio is little more than a place of refuge for aging Peter Pans. Schools all over the land, including some respected ones, are still "educating" thousands of painters to the level of proficient amateurism in the wake of the most successful current vogue. These amateurs go out to teach other amateurs to think of themselves as professional artists, and those with enough brass, luck and patronage enjoy professional status in the salesrooms.

Outside the market, our unsalable amateur-as-professional is supported by dozens of institutions dedicated to the idea that art is a delicate flower to be grown not with its roots in soil but in a chemical bath. University art departments are so eager to build themselves up that you may find a graduate school of painting with twenty candidates for advanced degrees, all living on fellowships.

After graduation, foundation after foundation offers room and board and a bit of pocket money to allow painters to produce more paintings that have no other reason for being than that their production gives satisfaction to the people

who paint them as a continuation of the old painting-experi-
ence of childhood. With good enough connections to write
letters of recommendation, a painter may live for years without selling a picture, and may be paid to paint more pictures than he can give away. One nice thing about children
is that they are seldom interested in saving their work unless
adults give them the idea that it is worth keeping.

Any painter capable of seeing beyond the end of his nose
and honestly willing to examine his work from a distance
might even ask himself whether he has substituted anything
for the quality of innocent expression and fortunate accident
that can bring children's art and some amateur art close
to the boundaries of true art. If he has substituted only the
manual control of his medium in the service of a manner,
he has not substituted enough. A bit of kinetic flair does not
make an artist. It never has. It never will. It can't. And no
amount of esoteric critical jargon, applied after the fact in
an effort to make a painting something that it isn't, can make
it anything but what it is except for the gullible.

May 8, 1960

PERHAPS DRASTIC:
A Proposal for a Moratorium on Art.

A letter of suspicious origin, since it is postmarked last week
yet bears the supposed signature of William Adolphe Bouguereau, a notoriously conservative painter who died in

1905, has been delivered to this department. It contains an interesting idea.

Referring to Labor Day as the New Year's Day of the New York season, the letter suggests that all artists resolve to produce no work for the ensuing twelvemonth and that all art galleries close, to give the art situation a chance to come into balance. It further suggests that if this moratorium is impossible to arrange on a man-to-man basis, legal measures be taken to effect it.

Preposterous at first glance, the scheme has much to recommend it upon closer examination, although Mr. Bouguereau, as he must be called, has jumped into things without a clear notion of the side issues involved in a course of action that, while it may seem simple to him, would actually be terribly complicated.

In the first place, a year might not be enough of a breather. We would need a temporary Volstead Act for the arts, to be rescinded only after it has served its purpose. Furthermore, if the measure were to be effective, not only should the production of a work of art be illegal after the date of enactment but also the purchase and ownership of any work of art so produced should be equally prohibited and punishable under law.

Penalties for violation would have to be heavy, so heavy that only artists with a true calling, willing to return to the grand old romantic tradition of the artist as a rebel against society, would dare risk them by working in secret. (Paints and brushes and canvas would still be sold, just as the ingredients and apparatus for the manufacture of home brew were sold during Prohibition, with the proviso that their use for that purpose was illegal.) Thus the number of artists would be reduced, overnight, to normal, and this handful would be working in something a little closer to normal conditions than they do now, when our mass hysteria for creative activity is encouraged on every hand.

Under such limitations, the vogue for collecting also would come back into balance, although a bit more slowly. Forced to sit around year after year with the same old paintings, deprived of the pleasure of showing their latest acquisition to friends, and with no prospect of selling in a rising market —with, in fact, the monetary value of their collections reduced to exactly nothing—collectors of contemporary art would begin to examine their possessions as works of art, and question them as such, rather than as prestige symbols.

The weeding out would be fantastic. To take care of this, the transportation of paintings to storage places would be legal and there would be a boom in the warehouse business. But storage prices would also be set by law and would be very high, forcing the collector to wonder whether the painting was worth holding on to at all. Vast quantities of smeared canvas would end in the incinerators, speeding up a process that is inevitable anyway.

As one examines the proposal, it seems better and better. Youth would benefit. Talented children growing up during the moratorium, denied a career in art and protected from infection in Saturday morning museum classes, would be directed into useful activities. The shortage of scientists and engineers would be alleviated. Painters too old for re-education would turn to the help-wanted columns. Accustomed to soft living in expensive surroundings as a result of today's art market, many would enter domestic service, learning their new profession from the few remaining specimens of a breed that is threatened with extinction.

Foundations now devoted to encouraging the arts could

reallocate their funds to set up emergency programs in domestic science with Mrs. Beeton's "The Book of Household Management" as a basic text at hand. The prospect of a buyer's market in butlers and upstairs maids would be, alone, enough to assure the popularity of the Art-Volstead Act with the moneyed class, who would be offered a solution to a real problem in their lives and would be happy to sacrifice to it the minor pleasure of collecting dubious works of art.

University art faculties would fill the higher brackets of domestic service. Intelligent and cultivated, they would be pleasant to have around the best houses. Everything would work out beautifully. No separation of married couples would be involved, for instance, since the couple in service is much sought after and is highly paid. Nor would there be the pain and inconvenience of geographical displacement, since the domestic servant problem is universal. The question of social downgrading, which at first would bother the wives of full professors, is more apparent than real.

In other fields, similarly happy solutions would present themselves. No financial hardship would be involved for the dealer. His first impulse might be to turn his gallery into an art speakeasy, yet this would be impractical and expensive, involving protective honorariums to members of a rough element of society. On second thought, dealers will realize that if they can sell some of the things people have been buying in recent years, they can sell anything. They will find some other commodity for which they can create a demand with the help of the same middlemen whose flexible loyalties serve them so well at present.

But if we are really to get our eyes back, the prohibition against exhibiting should extend to all works of art created during the last ten years, letting the good fall temporarily with the bad. The Museum of Modern Art, the Guggenheim and the Whitney might have to close for a few weeks to check the dates on their pictures and seal the prohibited ones in vaults. But the Museum of Modern Art complains that it has not room to exhibit some of its best things even now, and they could do so in the space ordinarily alloted to such breath-takers as last year's "Sixteen Americans."

As for the Guggenheim, it would still be in business if the walls were bare. The question as to whether the structure is architecture or a monument of abstract sculpture and hence illegal under the terms of the Act is a technical one and would have to be dealt with by a committee. It should not be the intention of the Act to create embarrassment or hardship for any individual or institution. But the Whitney, which lately has joined the tail of the Museum of Modern Art's game of follow-the-leader, might experience a slight trauma in being forced to drop back a decade and pick up its own game where it left off.

Happily, such questions would not arise for the Metropolitan Museum because its contemporary American paintings, purchased for mysterious reasons, have always been whisked into storage upon delivery. The Metropolitan would even have a boom, with lectures on "Understanding the Old Masters," since lectures on "Understanding Modern Art" would come within the prohibitions of the proposed Act, leaving a large and insatiable audience at loose ends.

The question remains of how to decide when the Act is to be rescinded. It should not be allowed to remain in force too long. After five years or so, some kind of equilibrium might already be apparent. After ten, the nature of this equilibrium should be recognizable, making possible a return to the studios on a cautious, carefully supervised tapering-on basis.

But without question many people formerly directly involved with the arts will have come to prefer their new circumstances, having established legitimate and respectable relationships to a more stable society.

Here, in fact, lies the danger of Mr. Bouguereau's suggestion. We must not be lulled by the peaceful world the Act would create. On the contrary, we must remain alert to avoid a prolongation of the moratorium beyond the point of no return. Give it twenty years and nobody would want to change the status quo it would create. No more art. Ever.

The present situation, out of kilter though it may be, isn't that bad. Before Mr. Bouguereau writes his Congressman, he should sit down and examine his proposal for every possibility it holds of permanent national cultural disaster as the price of temporary relief.

September 4, 1960

PART TWO:
Magic and Caprice

THE SEARCH FOR MAGIC:
Cave Art and Contemporary Art.

The other day they dug up a sliver of bone in the desert near Valsequillo, Mexico, that seems to be about 30,000 years old —part of the pelvis of an Ice Age elephant. While you don't dig up pieces of bone that old every day, there are plenty of them around. What made this one exceptional was that it had some drawings of animals scratched on it, and since animals don't go around scratching drawings of other animals on the bones of yet other animals, this meant that men as well as animals were alive 30,000 years ago on the North American continent.

The discovery made a difference in our estimate of the time of man's debut in these parts, back-dating it by 20,000 years (in round numbers), and it also showed us again something we already knew—that then, as now, man was busy with something we call art.

Esthetically these particular prehistoric scratchings, or engravings as they are properly called, are not world-beaters. No ideas about prehistoric art were revised as a result of their discovery. They look very much like the already well-known engravings and paintings by cave artists of the same period in Europe, except that they are cruder, indicating the possibility that even at that date America was a little behind Europe in the arts, a cultural lag that was still bothering Henry James when he wrote about Americans in Europe at the end of the nineteenth century A. D.

Anthropologically exciting, the discovery was artistically nothing much. But anyone who saw the enlarged photograph of the bone sliver in the newspapers may have been taken aback if he happened coincidentally to pay a visit to the

Guggenheim Museum or the Museum of Modern Art, where exhibitions of contemporary Spanish painting were then on view. The resemblance between the photograph of the 30,-000-year-old bone sliver and one school of contemporary art is close enough to jolt you out of all your comfortable notions about time sequences if you hold to the conventional concept of time as something that moves forward in a straight line out of the infinite past toward the infinite future.

Even while anthropologists were examining their discovery, critics were examining the Spanish paintings and were finding that one group of them resembled, more than anything else, portions of the areas of prehistoric cave walls excised from their natural locations and framed. The slab-like abstractions have the same rough texture, the same stony colors mottled as if by time, and are patterned with much the same kinds of lines, dug into thick paint, as those that were dug into bone or stone so long ago.

At first thought, this close resemblance might suggest that in the atomic age the modern artist, always a quick one to get in on the newest ground floor, has run for the caves, things having come 359 degrees toward full circle as civilization prepares to get rid of itself and start all over again. But, while a return to the shelter of the caves might be a sound course of action, it is not exactly what the artists have in mind.

Rather, the idea is that while we may have worked in a circular way through 30,000 years of art history to arrive more or less at the point from which we started, we have done it not on the flat, but on the upgrade, and from our superior level on the spiral we have a nice view of cave art way below us and have discovered that it has quite a bit of stuff in it that we can make use of.

This stuff is, in a word—magic.

To understand where the difference lies between the art of the caves and the modern art that looks so much like the art of the caves, but isn't, we have to remember first that although the men who decorated the cave walls were frequently what we would call artists—and superb ones—there is not much likelihood that they knew it. They could hardly have had a word (or a sound, or whatever it was that they used for communication) that meant what we mean when we say "art" or "artist" today, because there was no such concept to require the word.

Art as a diversion for an audience, art as an intellectual experience, art as self-expression, art as a means of relaying ideas or emotions from the artist to other individuals, art as ornament for purely visual enjoyment, art as the product of impulse, art for art's sake—art from this compound point of view, which is ours, did not exist.

Cave art may afford diversion for a twentieth-century audience and may be intellectually and emotionally stimulating to us. We can imagine its having been a self-expression for the men who created it. It is a vivid communication between us and the men of 30,000 years ago and it is breathtakingly ornamental.

By our terms, the artistry of the paintings in the Lascaux caves of central France is supreme and to see them is one of the great experiences the world has to offer. They are staggeringly evocative, and as a purely visual spectacle many people have found them at least as stunning as Michelangelo's Sistine Ceiling frescoes, which they resemble in color and to which they are often compared. But we are the ones who make them art, and we are the ones who make artists out of the men who painted them, in our sense of the words "art" and "artist."

Come to think of it, if the cave men could not have had a word for "art," we are short a word also. We have none except the inaccurate "artist" to mean "the-man-whose-job-it-is-to-make-the-magic-symbol-images-on-the-walls-of-the-place-of-ceremonies." The caves were not decorated habitations, but places for rituals, and the images that cover them were not put there to look pretty, but to serve specific magical and religious purposes.

Some anthropologists believe that the cave artist was treated as a man with special duties that excused him from the hunting that took most of the time of other men. He shared their kills, which was fair enough since the man-made images he created gave men power over the animals they hunted. The idea persists in voodoo today: a waxen image of your enemy, after proper arrangements with a dependable voodoo practitioner, can be melted down with disastrous results to the victim of your choice.

No doubt the cave artist was right up in there with the best hunters, the best chippers of axes and spearheads, and with other individuals who best performed the duties upon which existence depended. But we have no reason to think that he was thought of, as we think of our artists, as an individual subject to fits of inspiration brought on by visitations of the Divine Fire. He was first of all a man who did what he did as a function of tribal life.

Our ideas about the position of the artist in the tribe must be conjectural, but the surest conjecture of all is that in a rough, hard and dangerous world, where every man had to pull his own weight, there was no ivory tower for any man, no time for theorizing about esoteric knickknacks, no place for a work of art that didn't make sense to everybody and, above all, no place for a work of art that wasn't created for a specific and necessary purpose.

Now, the best thing that an artist can ask of life is that his work be needed, wanted, demanded. Ivory towers are usually inhabited as makeshifts for better quarters, and our modern artists, forced into them, have not always found them comfortable. They tend to be chilly, they are difficult for your friends to get to, and they are impossible to ventilate. The one thing they offer in unlimited supply is privacy, but this can also be said in favor of solitary confinement.

From the ivory tower, the caves look good. But this is no sudden discovery. For three-quarters of a century now, the most sophisticated artists, in a world where art has come to occupy a dubious position, have increasingly drawn sustenance from the art of primitive peoples in whose worlds art was not cultivated for art's sake but was demanded to fulfill direct and definable purposes.

In the eighteen eighties and nineties, when Gauguin went first to the primitive villages of Brittany and then to the more primitive islands of the South Seas, he was interested partly in picturesque local color, but much more in survivals of the kind of mystical superstition to which primitive civilizations have always given tangible expression. In the next decade, Matisse, Picasso and a crowd of others "discovered" African tribal sculpture, and although the use they made of it was intellectual, part of its inherent attraction was its vigorous evocation of a world where art was still the natural and full expression of fundamental, unquestioned concepts.

This identification of art with the basic forces in the society that produces it is tremendously appealing in a century when art has become more and more divorced from life; when it must even be created, as often as not, in actual opposition to the forces of life that animate the world outside the studio—a world where, at best, a kind of art and a kind of life are joined in a shaky liaison synthesized by museums and dealers who are dedicated to this kind of matchmaking between lonely hearts.

But the idea that artists prefer this situation to a healthier one is erroneous. There is hardly an artist, even among those whose art seems most esoteric to the layman, who will not say, and mean it, that, rather than retreating from life, he is trying to isolate some quality that is most fundamental in it. Few succeed. Relatively few, for that matter, have succeeded in any age, but the modern world has made the artist's frustrations intense. The more he intellectualizes, the more he discovers that eventually he bumps into the old function of the artist as a kind of necromancer.

Hence the return, on the part of more artists every day, to faith in the oldest idea of all, the idea of art as the creation of magical symbols through which man relates himself to his environment. The artist no longer believes that these symbols will be of actual physical help. That is, they will not help him to kill a bison or to find a taxi at the rush hour. But they help him in his exploratory examinations of a problem everybody faces today—how to stay sane and purposeful in a world of science that explains everything to the intellect yet leaves the spirit baffled.

The current generation of Spaniards has an immediate precedent in Joan Miró, called by many critics one of the three determining artists of the twentieth century (the others being Matisse and Picasso). For thirty-five years Miró has been filling his canvases with curious beasts, monsters, demons, spooks and cryptographic signs that would not be out of place in prehistoric caves if cave art had developed, let us say, a rococo period. In France, Jean Dubuffet, whose position is more important year by year, paints images that are completely of the twentieth century, yet are more suggestive of appeals to timeless dark spirits than of rationalizations of contemporary experience.

Both Miró and Dubuffet have also done sculptures recalling idols, mystical even while brutal and perverse. And lately Miró has turned to ceramics, as if yearning to abandon the canvas for a return to the stone wall.

In 1958 he completed for UNESCO headquarters in Paris a ceramic wall 10 feet high and 25 feet long that makes him a good representative of the artist-come-full-circle after 30,000 years. Called "Night" and composed of a recognizable moon, a half-recognizable star, and some unrecognizable symbols, it would probably have been less puzzling to the cave artists than it is to 90 per cent of the tourists who wonder about it today.

But the artist of widest influence in this field is Paul Klee. Dead these twenty years, Klee was the first advocate of modern magic. He intellectualized with the best of them, but he produced fantasies that drew heavily on the forms of primitive art. Of all that he said and wrote, the summary is that "art in the highest sense" deals with an "ultimate mystery [that] lies behind the ambiguity which the light of the intellect fails miserably to penetrate."

The modern artist's dilemma has been stated in many ways, but never better than that. For the artist as for the rest of us, the "ultimate mystery," for which one name is the soul, remains the most important thing in the world, and the one inexplicable thing in a world dedicated to explaining everything by science. Thirty thousand years ago we used to give souls, friendly or evil, to other things in the world—to trees, to water, to the wind, to rocks. In our hearts we continued to hold on to the idea after we knew better. Even in the very early years of this century it was possible to speak of your "soul communing with nature" without being laughed at.

But today the soul has been robbed of its companions, and since everything else has been explained away from the mystical values we used to think existed, we have begun to feel— rationally—that perhaps this mystery of the spirit never existed at all, that it, too, will soon be explained away. But —irrationally—we still believe in it, and art is one place where we look for proof of it.

Science applied to art can never be more than pseudo-science or at best an adjunct to the thing art is really about, magic. Before the invention of photography there was a kind of magic to even the most realistic, the most prosaic image. It was the magic of the transformation of a three dimensional world into a two dimensional illusion. But science has robbed us here as elsewhere. Physics and chemistry, combined in photography, have glutted us with images and so associated them with a mechanical process that the magic is gone.

And here, of course, is where the artist's problem lies. Since he must invent new forms, it may be as difficult for him to reach people with his magic as it has been impossible for him to reach them with his intellectualized abstractions. And reach us, somehow, he must—for magic is meaningless unless we are allowed to participate in its rituals.

We have no vocabulary of magical symbols today. In pre-historic and primitive art every line, circle or cross, as well as every recognizable form, was engraved or painted or carved as it was because the artist, and the tribe, knew what it symbolized and believed in its power. But today the artist's symbols are perforce a private vocabulary in which he continues to talk to himself. The gap between the contemporary painter and the contemporary public is so wide that we can hardly tell whether any first step is in the direction of closing it, or off on another tangent.

Are the new painters, who are apparently interested in magic, just capitalizing on a new set of textures, a new set of curious forms, a new set of novelties, as so many contemporary painters have done for so long to achieve the kind of cocktail-success that endures only as long as it titillates? Or are they really hoping to reach us, and are they willing to meet at least half way a public that so far has been asked to make all the concessions?

In other words, the question is whether the artist will succeed only in doing magic tricks in the drawing room, or whether he will bring back to art the true magic in which, irrationally, we continue to believe, the mysteries to which art, until our century, has always given proof. If the artist can find new ways to evoke once more the responses that are buried deep within the rest of us, he will have made a start toward somewhere—perhaps along the next round of the spiral.

October 16, 1960

THE MOUTHS OF BABES:
Children's Art.

Every fall when some five or six million American youngsters
enter the first grade as candidates for initiation into the mysteries of reading, writing and arithmetic, a large percentage
of them are already veterans in the practice of the greatest
mystery of all—art. Some have explored independently with
their paint boxes on paper, or their chalk on sidewalks, or
with sticks in the dust or on the damp sand of the beach.
Others have been assisted in the transition from playpen to
studio by teachers in playschool and kindergarten. Some who
live in cities with museums have extended their studies in the
proximity, but not in the manner, of the masters.

Children are masters in their own way, and the chances
are that the museum where they attend classes has a collection of children's art. Mamas and papas used to be the only
such collectors, on the sole basis of parental sentiment. But
today not only museums but also art collectors, artists, art
historians, sociologists, psychiatrists, philosophers and people
who just plain like pictures, are likely to have their cache
of art by children to whom they are no more related than
they are to Leonardo da Vinci.

Why do children paint, and how? And why has our century been the first to have recognized children's art as something more than quaint and cute? As a start on an answer,
let us look in on a class.

Our special interest is an artist aged five. He and the paint-

Child drawing on beach. Photograph by Burt Chernow, Greens Farms School, Westport, Connecticut.

ing we will describe are not imaginary, but the locale—best described as a room stripped for action—need not be specific. It could be in any museum, art center, or public or private school in this country where the art of children is understood and respected.

The teacher is a young woman who qualifies for the job because she likes children and they like her, and because she knows that the basic approach in teaching the very young artist is to issue the paint rations and jump quickly out of range. She also knows enough about painting to offer helpful suggestions to a stalled fellow artist when advisable. Above all, she abhors the old colorbook idea for what it is, pointless at least and usually throttling to the imagination as well. She never in her life gave a child someone else's picture to color, and she would sooner cut her tongue out than tell him to be neat and stay within the lines.

Each of her students straddles his own low bench, facing a board at one end to which a piece of cheap paper about 20 x 24 inches is thumbtacked. He is supplied with a large, soft-haired brush, a muffin baking pan holding half a dozen pools of thick liquid colors in its compartments, and a generous pitcher of water. He is smocked, often in one of his father's old shirts, worn backwards.

Since this is not the first meeting of the class, the children have arrived knowing what they want to paint this time, and the group gets down to business with an alacrity that keeps the teacher busy issuing new paper as ideas are tossed off and the completed works discarded. However, some less athletic painting is also going on, and our five-year-old's approach happens to be deliberate and reflective, though vigorous and decisive.

He fills his brush from the yellow puddle, spreads a generous quantity in a circle in the center of the paper, and enlarges it ring by ring until it runs off all four edges and the paper is a solid yellow.

Remembering to rinse out his brush, he next heads for the green, and applies a band of that color across the lower two or three inches of the picture. Then he paints a corresponding blue band across the top. Both colors get mixed up here and there with the yellow, and there is a bit of dribbling, but none of this bothers him. He understands the nature of his medium.

He now sits still for a while, contemplating his production, not from pride or to size things up or even to let the paint dry. He simply has the air of waiting during an interval between events, an interval that is part of the conception of the picture.

This interval is concluded after thirty seconds or so, and he takes the blue again and pulls a series of lines out of the top band until they touch the green band at the bottom. These lines very nearly cover the portion of the picture on which they are painted, and they are always drawn from the blue band downward.

The picture is now nearly completed. As a final episode, our artist washes his brush again, dips it into the black, and covers the entire surface, obscuring everything.

What happened here was that the sun rose and its light spread. The light revealed a green earth, over which there was a blue sky. The morning remained sunny. That afternoon it rained. Then it was night, and you couldn't see anything any more.

Throughout this performance the artist exhibited a fine independence from borrowed ideas and a great directness in getting to the heart of things. What is the sun? A great ball of light. We have seen its rays represented as radiating spokes, but this is a convention, and this child ignored it to make the light spread out in all directions from the ball, filling all space, as of course it does.

Like any child who has not been taught to do otherwise, he put the green earth at the bottom and the blue sky at the top and left a great gap in between, since of course there is a gap between earth and sky. This stuff about their meeting at the horizon is a sophistication and, literally, an illusion. When children paint they deal not with illusion but with truth, not with optics but with fact. The rain fell as it should, down from the sky until it hit the earth. And what is night?

Blackness, concealing everything. The green earth is still there, under the black, but you can't see it. Naturally.

As a natural artist, a child conceives of a picture not as a predetermined entity but as an exploration, and he explores on his own terms without questioning whether the shapes and colors he puts down are as legible to others as they are to him. When he begins to worry about how his picture is going to look to someone else, it means that an inhibiting teacher has planted the question or that he is no longer a child in his way of responding to the world.

But the description of the child as a "natural artist" raises an interruptive query: if children are natural artists, was Rubens (for instance) an unnatural one?

Certainly he was. All artists are unnatural to the extent that their knowledge, their technique, their thought about what they are doing, goes beyond the definition of "natural" as "from, or by, birth; innate, inborn." Children are natural artists because they paint or draw or dance or sing in response to inner promptings. When established conventions begin to dominate this prompting, the natural artist's period of esthetic innocence is over.

A child's innate, inborn impulse toward art manifests itself in its most familiar elementary form on that day when the toddler discovers that daddy's pencil does fascinating things to mommy's wall if you apply the point firmly and walk the length of the room moving your arm up and down. A similar kinetic exuberance continues to determine his style after his energies are redirected from the impromptu mural to the blackboard or the informal easel painting, and it is a rare child who, unless these impulses are thwarted or badly directed, never turns out a bit of interesting work between the ages of four and ten.

Between the day of the wall scribble and the first glimmer of conventional adult social awareness, there are a few wonderful years when children take to brush and paint like young animals discovering their habitat—air, water or woods. And they are, by analogy, discovering their habitat—not the physical one that surrounds them, but the uniquely human habitat of interpretative responses that differentiate men from animals and, hence, children from puppies, kittens or cubs. As succinct a statement of the difference between men and animals as you could find might be "Animals don't draw."

Unaware that there is any such thing as "self-expression," the child expresses himself with a directness that is the despair of many an adult artist. Interested in no formal problems of design, hampered by no criteria of technical performance, the child is fascinated simply by what happens when you make your own pictures of things. Because he is new to this world and busy discovering the first things about it, his art deals with an area of common truth that falls into expressive images both ancient and current, both universal and personal.

The very young child's stick-man with a circle for a head and lines for the torso, two arms, and two legs, is as old as the first drawing of a man, and still just as direct and clear. In every culture and in every country it has always been and always will be recognizable as the generic man, and when it stands on a band of green under a band of blue it means man in nature.

The forms of a more confusing world, a world filled with houses, trains, airplanes, streets, skyscrapers and television antennae, a world that is the natural one for the child today, are expressed in children's art with equal force and simplified truth. Because brick houses are reddish, a child paints them an honest, pure red. He reduces clothing, now a part of the natural man, to exactly what it is—a casing with buttons. Whatever he draws, a child gets to the heart of things by a natural recognition of those fundamentals for which mature artists search, and a natural indifference to the incidentals that obscure them.

Granted, of course, that the child's world is simpler than ours. But artists of such stature as Miró and Klee have studied the art of children and have learned from it. The twentieth century's explorations of the vagaries of the human mind have taught us that even our random doodlings on the telephone pad may be clues to aspects of personality of which we are unconscious. In the same way, the art of children affords signposts to an inner world we all share and have shared with thousands upon thousands of generations since the emergence of man on earth.

It is true that in our enthusiasm for interpreting it we often read things into children's art that the child had no intention of putting there. But even if we do, our responses may open up areas of our lives that we tend to close off. This is particularly true when we read children's art as fantasy. An imaginative child, when he paints, makes no distinction between what he imagines and what physically exists. He never hesitates to paint a man blue if for some reason that seems appropriate—or fun—to him. He represents one person walking and another person flying without suggesting that one form of locomotion is less usual than the other, although he will make it clear that flying is more fun.

The child's rudimentary technique is part and parcel of the expression of his rudimentary but significant experience of the world—of two worlds, in fact. His crude way of representing things is an advantage to him and a revelation to us not only because it hits hard at main points, but also because it is the perfect vehicle for picturing the dual but wonderfully unified regions of inner and outer experience in which we all live, but between which he has not yet set up barriers. The devices he hits upon in drawing and coloring his pictures give an air of fantasy to subjects he regards as factual, while his unquestioning representation of an imaginary world, presented by the same devices, identifies it with his world of visual fact.

The elimination of the dividing line between these two worlds has been a concern of artists before now and has dominated whole schools of contemporary painting. Hence if you are convinced that the forms and colors in children's art are dictated by some deep, natural expressive impulse, they offer clues to kinds of expression that are impossible in terms of conventional painting.

Only an artist who is also a fool would think that by imitating the art of children he can get any further than, say, a speaker who chooses to deliver his address in babytalk. But at the same time, the contemporary painter has felt stifled under the overlay of expert technical conventions accumulated during the centuries. He has sought ways out of what seems to him a dead end, ways to reach the truest emotional images rather than the most accurate visual ones. Since children seem to create exactly such images spontaneously, modern artists have tried to adapt these images to the infinitely complicated and subtle exploration of states of mind.

They don't always make the grade, and even when they do, the superficial resemblance to children's art may be strong enough to inspire lay observers to the familiar "My six-year-old boy could do better than that." What could be legitimately said is, "My six-year-old boy showed him how to begin that," which is a different thing altogether.

What happens to children's painting when they grow older? To some degree it can be directed and controlled, enlarged in scope. But the rule is that the purity of the first impulse fades as the child, now no longer quite a child, begins to size up the world in less direct terms. More often than not, he loses interest in this form of expression. For most children it serves its purpose and dies as naturally as it was born. When it endures into the immediately pre-adolescent years, the child begins to mistrust his own efforts and to compare them with adult art as a standard.

Esthetically, the change is as distressing as pimples. The delightful child-artist becomes only an incompetent non-adult artist worrying about representational accuracy and technical niceties. You would think that such considerations would mean less to children today than they used to, before so many modern artists abandoned realistic styles. But children are apparently pretty square in their ideas about art once they lose their esthetic innocence. Their standards are determined by the art they see most of, which is related to the things that are becoming most important to them. This means the art of magazine covers, advertisements, and illustrations. The one-time child artist does not shift from innocence to the sophistications of modern art to which, paradoxically, he has so importantly contributed.

In girls, one of the most usual symptoms of artistic decline is a preoccupation with realistic renditions of brides in meticulously designed wedding dresses. A thesis could be written on the difference between a bride who happens to pop up as part of a picture by a young child of either sex (perhaps there has been a wedding in the family) and a bride as pictured by a girl who is pondering the subject in a new light. The title could be "Transition from General Idea-Symbology to Particularized Reference in Bride Drawings by Pre-Adolescents," and by implication it could tell the whole story of where child artists come from and into what regions they vanish.

Horses also appear conspicuously in the feminine art syndrome at this stage, as do ballet dancers. But while the girls are off on such tacks, the boys at the same age either abandon art altogether or become absorbed in acutely detailed schemes for the construction of racing cars, sailboats, and space rockets.

Boys, too, may draw horses on occasion, but none has ever been known to draw a bridegroom.

August 27, 1961

THEIR HEART BELONGS TO DADA:
The Cult of the Irrational (Black Tie).

Plenty of people over the past fifty years or so, confronted by one concoction or another of the contemporary creative spirit, have asked indignantly, "Do you call *that* art?" But only one group of artists during those decades has been ready with the answer, "Certainly not," to confound the questioner further.

They were the dadaists, a disruptive band of esthetic stuntsmen, at once clowning and despairing, the only artists in the history of art to declare themselves anti-art and to devote their energies to the annihilation of all art values. They appeared simultaneously in several countries during World War I and continued their shenanigans into the early twenties.

Dada's best-known stunt, and one of its most typical, was the refurbishing of the Mona Lisa (in a photograph) with a neat little mustache and a goatee, plus a title in the form of an indecent French pun. This kind of irreverence for the past, of esthetic lawlessness, had its parallel in many another aspect of life in the twenties. In its own way, the American jazz age expressed the same flouting of past values and disrespect for the conventions, and the laws, of society.

A few years ago dada seemed as much a period piece as the flapper and the hip flask. But suddenly it is with us again, and going strong. So are the rest of the twenties in, for instance, the humorous revivals of musical comedies, which a middle-aged generation watches with a combination of recognition and incredulity. But dada's revival is taking place at another level. It is flourishing in the avant-garde galleries, in the current-trend exhibitions at the Museum of Modern Art, and in the international biennials everywhere. And its audience is pretty serious about the whole business.

In line with the original dada techniques, the neo-dadaists are making paste-ups of such detritus as shattered umbrellas, busted zippers, tangled string and discarded pillow stuffing, fragments of photographs, lace doilies ruined in the laundry, and just about anything else, including bits of things that have become unrecognizable in the process of disruption and decay. They are creating sculpture from wood or metal junk picked up in city dumps or the wreckage of buildings, and are constructing art machines, also from junk, that

Bruce Conner: *FEBRUARY 26 1959*. 18″ x 13″. Mixed media. Collection of Charles Alan, New York.

turn, wiggle, squawk, and even stagger around a bit under their own power.

At least one stuffed goat, with a rubber tire around its middle, has been offered for esthetic appraisal—and for sale, a far from incidental consideration. You may also buy, just now, a real wire coat hanger on a wooden peg projecting from a color-dabbed panel, if this appeals to you as something you would like to have around the house or if you think its value as an investment is likely to increase.

Since there is an explanation for everything—even for dada, the cult of the irrational—the dada revival suggests several questions, particularly the one, "How come?" You won't find the answer in the present work of the original dadaists who, having survived the excesses of their youth, are now in their seventies and respectably established as the patriarchs of modern art. They are no longer interested, as they once were, in entertaining themselves and outraging the public by exhibiting such objects as a urinal entitled "Fountain" or a miter box combined with a plumbing trap entitled "God."

As littérateurs they no longer write poems by picking words at random out of hats, nor as artists do they any longer compose designs by tearing a piece of paper into bits, letting the bits fall onto another piece of paper, and pasting them in place. They are not even interested in continuing one of their more painstaking techniques, which consisted of taking botanical or anatomical engravings, retouching them and giving them such titles as "The Gramineous Bicycle Garnished with Bells the Dappled Fire Damps and the Echinoderms Bending the Spine to Look for Caresses."

All such high jinks the old-line dadaists have put behind them. They spend their time playing chess or working in styles, usually abstract, that followed dada and that they helped to originate. The crew-cut or mop-haired neo-dada yearlings who now capitalize on dada's innovations of forty years ago are a different breed. Ask them the usual question, "Do you call that art?" and they are likely to forget and answer, "Of course."

This makes a world of difference. Perverse, shrill, insolent and shrewdly self-seeking dada may have been in the old days, but its antics were genuinely revolutionary. Its tomfoolery was inspired by genuine anger. It was dedicated to the destruction of all logical art values, both traditional and contemporary, because in a world that was totally illogical—as proved, the dadaists argued, by the 1914-18 war and its social aftermath—only the illogical could be expressive. The idea behind dada was that the function of art, which had always been to make sense out of the chaotic material of human experience, was outmoded along with the idea that sense could be made of anything any more. Hence, dada was dedicated to non-sense and was anti-art.

So, for all its mocking and japing and capering, dada was an art of despair. It was a comic song, a burlesque skit, a tricky dance by performers who felt that they and everybody else in the world were existing on top of a thin crust that might crumble at any time and plunge them into the ultimate abyss. One explanation offered for dada's revival is that the crust today is even thinner and the abyss beneath it even more horrible than the one hinted at by the First World War. Is the revival a natural nihilistic protest in response to a desperate state of affairs? Not quite.

In fact, not by a long shot. The old dada boys were on the soapbox and were greeted with the catcalls they invited. The new ones are safely in the drawing room, where they are assured of the approval of the audience to be found there today, an audience not only habituated to novelty but avid for it, not only respectful of new ideas but so eager to be diverted that it will accept any idea that presents itself as new.

Old-time dada could—and did, as it intended—provoke to fury. The imitators today only tease and titillate. It was one thing, in 1920, to be hit in the face with an idea during the intellectual free-for-all of those years. It is another, in 1960, to find the same idea served up as garnish on a platter of hors d'oeuvres at a fashionable reception.

Neo-dada's most engaging stunt to date is the "self-destroying work of art," and a select audience gathered recently at the Museum of Modern Art to watch one of these machines do away with itself. With considerable help from its builder, a Swiss named Jean Tinguely, the contraption—made of bicycle wheels, old bottles, an ancient upright piano, a toy wagon, and other miscellaneous scrap—managed to saw, beat and burn itself to death.

In itself, the idea of the self-destroying work of art is the cleverest and most appropriate postscript to the nihilistic spirit of dada, but the curious and doubly paradoxical feature of the event was that it was sponsored by an art museum and witnessed by the most important collectors and patrons of modern art in a city that has been generous beyond all precedent to contemporary experiments.

The theme of the evening—that the best thing to do with art is to get rid of it—probably caused no serious soul-searching when the collectors went home to their non-self-destroying collections, but it did leave many people with the feeling that dada might better have been left in its grave than brought to life for the purpose of suicide. Thus, in staging the show the museum performed its function as a place for the airing and examination of such questions as "What now?" and "What next?" although the answer was a bit unexpected.

Actually, the real dada's contribution to modern art has been considerable, and can be analyzed in positive rather than negative terms without too much forcing, if you are willing to accept in the first place the premise that the world is in a really bad way.

As one instance, a whole school of contemporary sculptors works by gathering together parts of junked machines and welding them into new forms, sometimes eerily suggestive of monstrous creatures, more often simply abstract structures existing without reference to natural—or unnatural—forms of nature.

An old automobile exhaust pipe, part of a boiler, some cogs and the like may never be anything but a pipe, a part of a boiler, and some cogs to the obtuse layman. Nevertheless, it is possible to regard them as pure shapes, with their special colors and textures, and to combine them in an arrangement that has its own character esthetically.

Just where stunts end and art begins in these reclaimed-junk constructions is hard to say. But accept, for the moment, the contention that this kind of thing can work, esthetically. It does for many people. In that case, the artist has taken parts of broken machines, like the parts of our broken civilization and, by making them make some kind of sense, has salvaged something from our universal rubbish heap. This is hardly the kind of high idealism that the average person expects from art, but for the dada-derived artist, whose philosophical point of departure is despair, the statement is relatively optimistic.

One of the original dadaists, Kurt Schwitters, who died

in 1948, worked for ten years on a structure of "found objects," as such bits of metal, wood, cork or what-have-you are called. It grew so large that it finally pierced the three floors of his house—but was destroyed in the Second World War. He began two others, neither of which was he able to finish before his death.

Schwitters' long-term dedication went beyond the overnight stunts of dada and, in this case, the resultant work moved from dada into another field called constructivism. (Schwitters was, in fact, disinherited by the dadaists as "reactionary.") Such are the multiple overlappings and vaguely defined divisions of modern art.

It is probable, also—although they would probably deny it—that the abstract-expressionist painters who create their effects by dripping, dribbling and flinging paint on canvas also have a source in dada. Dada put great faith in accident, as the ultimate denial of logic. Even its name, which is French baby talk for "horse" or a colloquial word meaning any hobby or idea that one is downright foolish over, is supposed to have been chosen by opening a dictionary at random—in spite of its suspicious appropriateness. The paint drippers, dribblers and flingers are manipulators of "controlled accidents," and although the word "controlled" is the important one, the faith in accident, in this case for personal expression, is still there.

At this point we may find the best explanation for dada's revival. Purely abstract art has been in the ascendant long enough now for its original fans to be ready to question it, and for its purely spectator audience to weary of it. It long ago descended from the stratosphere of pure intellectualism into the somewhat lower realm of fashionable popularity, and lately it has dropped even further, into advertising and the feature pages of mass-circulation journals, so that it is on the edge of becoming commonplace instead of chic.

Something else is needed for a chic audience, but a return to conventional realism is still considered impossible, and a vague concept called "the new realism" or "the new reality" is in the air. Essentially, this idea is that even an abstract painting may have the "reality" of its materials. If the paint is so thick that you can literally take hold of it, or if various other immediately tangible materials are incorporated into it, you have realism of a kind even more direct than the realism of painted images that imitate nature.

Neo-dada offers this kind of tangibility. Modern art's audience, which would see no point in the technical skill involved in painting a lace doily in detail, is fascinated to find a real lace doily incorporated into a dada concoction. The avant-garde that would regard an illusionistically painted button as reactionary is happy enough to accept real buttons sewed onto a canvas and framed.

There is just a chance—maybe—that this kind of realism might suggest to a super-avant-garde painter, one day, that the time, skill and patience involved in realistic painting might constitute a new kind of novelty, and in that case dada might lead to—of all things—a new kind of naturalism. If this should happen, it would be the fatal paradox for an art that just now depends on one paradox after another for its life. And it would not be the first time that dada failed by making sense in spite of itself. Many an artist who tries to make sense ends up by making none, but dada's history shows how hard it is to be meaningless when you work at it.

The original movement met its death in Paris when

Freudian interpretations gave meaning to apparently irrational fantasies. Dada merged with surrealism, the art of
illustration for Freudian dream manuals, and as an independent movement it was finished. Before long its anti-
art was conspicuously enshrined in museums of modern art.
Dada nonsense was embalmed as a period-piece expression
of a disturbed time, and the movement was entered in the
history books with an official death date of 1922.

One thing you can depend on, however, is that any art
movement that has been a good thing at one time will be
exhumed at another and examined for reuse. The original
dada lasted as long as it concerned its inventors. How long
will the revival go on? Probably as long as it amuses the
customers.

June 5, 1960

ART AND DESTRUCTION:
Thoughts Following a Suicide in a Garden.

Jean Tinguely's machine called "Homage to New York,"
characterized as "a self-destroying work of art," which limped
to its demise before a selected audience in the garden of
the Museum of Modern Art on the evening of March 17,
1960, was a bizarre contraption indeed, born of Despair
out of Impertinence, if I understand its geneology. It reflected, as a work of art must do willy-nilly, an aspect of
its time, but did so by plan.

"Homage to New York" measured 23 feet long by 27 feet high before it began making trouble for itself, and it was an object of perverse attraction if not of classical beauty, a super-gadget constructed of such elements as eighty bicycle, tricycle and wagon wheels, an already moribund player piano, a battered toy wagon, an enameled bathtub, a meteorological trial balloon, many glass bottles, and other material picked up in junk yards. Powered by fifteen motors, it was designed to beat, burn, hammer and saw itself to death, although it proved to be not well enough constructed to do so without help. During the process it made music of a kind, produced abstract paintings in caricature of the "action" school, erased them, and even procreated in the form of a segment that, detaching itself from the parent machine, had the power of independent locomotion.

After some emergency mid-wifery performed by Mr. Tinguely, this little monster actually did hobble away for a few paces, with a gait altogether grotesque, hilarious, and eerie. Finally, after more human intervention than a good machine bent on suicide should require, the end was obviously near and the coup de grâce was administered by a fireman with an extinguisher.

Some of the implications of the self-destroying machine as a work of art, which make it more than a stunt, would include, in the field of social comment, the gesture of independence against machines in a world they are beginning to control. And as an essay in criticism, taking as its subject the transient and inchoate nature of much contemporary art, the machine made its point trenchantly, even if somewhat unfairly by means of reduction to absurdity.

But without tracing these ideas further, just now, we might give a thought to the persistence of destruction as a factor in the ideology of the artist in the twentieth century. Certainly this is peculiar to him in contrast with artists of other centuries, for only by the most precious forcing can we pretend that until our time art was anything but unquestioningly dedicated to the general ideal of capturing, holding and ordering the life and thought of man.

Our preoccupation with destruction has a positive facet of sorts in the effort of the twentieth-century artist to clear his decks of a past that has piled up for so long that he feels stifled under it. The futurists, in 1909, advocated tearing down all institutions devoted to the preservation of the past, such as museums, libraries and schools, a suggestion that failed to catch on. A more significant kind of destruction, however, was already taking place in cubism, not as a program of destruction as a policy, but incidentally in the course of experiments branching out in one direction from the art of Cézanne.

This was the destruction of the pictorial image as art had always known it in one form or another—"form" in a double sense here—by shattering it into multitudinous planes, planes that, in effect, have never been reassembled in their pre-cubist relationship. No painter who has passed through the experience of cubism, even vicariously as is the case with young painters today, can ever again see a solid object as pre-cubist painters saw it.

But this was not the end. "I think," wrote Mondrian in the margin of a letter to James Johnson Sweeney in 1943, "the destructive element is too much neglected in art." Mondrian objected to cubism as an art that intended to express volume, even in a new way, since this was opposed to his contention that volume had to be destroyed. The way to destroy volume is to paint in a single plane, which Mondrian

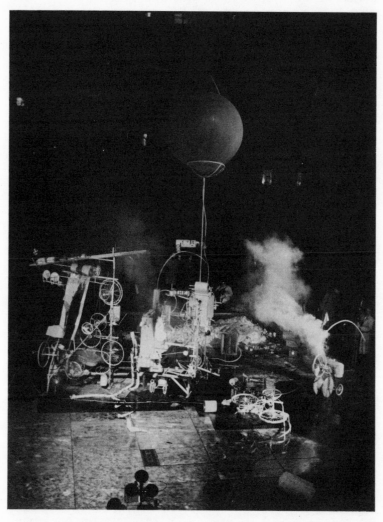

JEAN TINGUELY: *"HOMAGE TO NEW YORK" destroying itself in the garden of The Museum of Modern Art, New York, March 17, 1960.* Photograph by Allyn Baum, *The New York Times.*

did in compositions of flat rectangles defined by precise
horizontal and vertical lines. Mondrian next set out, he said,
to destroy the lines defining the rectangles by creating mu-
tual oppositions between them.

This process must seem one of progressively diminishing
returns except to the esthetician, for whom it affords a stimulating exercise in theory, or for the art historian, who sees
behind each Mondrian, so to speak, the whole story of which
the spare and ultra-refined painting is the end result. But
this kind of destruction, as Mondrian called it, or purification
or distillation as it could be called, was destruction toward a
goal, and above all an exercise in logic tempered by highly
developed sensitivities to formal values.

Destruction of another kind, the destruction of logic or at
least its avoidance, is represented by painters who could say
with Nicolas de Staël, "I believe in the accidental. As soon
as I sense a logic, too much logic, I become unnerved, and
naturally tend towards the illogical." And in an article of
interest to any painter, the introduction to the Winter, 1960,
issue of *Daedalus,* the journal of the American Academy
of Arts and Sciences, Gyorgy Kepes writes of the artist who
is most destructive of all, the contemporary painter or sculptor who speaks in "idioms in tune with the twilight spirit
that created them: surfaces that are moldy, broken, cor-
roded, ragged, dripping; brush strokes executed with the
sloppy brutality of cornered men"; of artists who are "dis-
placed persons who tour the inner ruins much as, in the last
century, the Romantics toured the ruins of the outside
world"; who have "made a central principle of the unformed,
the irrational, and the uncontrolled" and have created an
"image" that is "reduced to the elementary experience of the
kinesthetic pleasure of the act of painting."

Mr. Kepes is not commenting on abstract art, but on one aspect of contemporary art that happens to be abstract. He does not use the terms, but he is referring to a kind of painting that falls within the boundaries of abstract expressionism and "action painting," which except in their most glowing moments are not only the most destructive art of all, but also the most vicious, because the destructive principle is mistaken for a constructive one by the artists.

It is at this point that Mr. Tinguely's art begins to make sense. The reason I was impressed by his foolish and ill-constructed machine was that it had a perverse honesty. Like the dadaists before him—and he really does not do much more than elaborate upon them, he is not really inventive but only ingenious—Mr. Tinguely admits that mankind is licked.

Dada was a cult of unreason, an escape into nihilism, but a frank, even a declared one. Witnessing World War I—and how much more we have witnessed since then!—the dadaists seemed to say that if millennia of efforts to apply reason and logic could bring men to no better pass, then reason and logic must be abandoned. This is despair—a deadly sin and the only unforgivable one when magnified to its theological definition.

But for the dadaist, including the current crop of neo-dadaists in the flourishing revival, despair may be assuaged by the act of negative creation, the creation of objects that offend others by denying hope, that shock them and thus affirm the personality of the despairer. It is an immature point of view, related to adolescent rebellion and to the impulse that leads Oxford undergraduates to risk their necks in climbing at night to put chamberpots on top of the university's Gothic spires. But it is nevertheless a point of view less self-deceiving than many.

Mr. Tinguely received an ovation upon the death of his machine. Within the limits of dada he deserved it. By a more demanding standard he deserved a nod of recognition for an elaborate witticism on a subject of deadly seriousness, man's loss of faith.

March 27, 1960

THE BLIND ARTIST:

In a Crucial Time, He Plays at Games.

Coincidence with international events of supreme importance cast a disastrous light last week on the opening of "New Media—New Forms: Version II" at the Martha Jackson Gallery. At a time when the front page is filled with the kind of news it is just now, a show like this one is downright embarrassing.

The gallery is on Sixty-ninth Street near Madison Avenue, and to get there by bus from downtown last week you had to push your way through crowds of demonstrators and their audience at the corner of Forty-third and Madison. These particular demonstrators were behaving in a sober manner. They looked intelligent and determined as they held their placards above the crowd. The police, half a dozen on horseback and a dozen or so on foot, were firm and polite to the crowds that wanted to stop and watch. "Move on please. No loitering please. Move on."

Once you got on the bus, you progressed up Madison Avenue by degrees more slowly than usual, in fits and starts between ways cleared for police escorts, their red lights flashing and their sirens crying and followed by black limousines carrying personages to the United Nations. Parts of several cross streets in the area of the gallery itself were closed off. Their short vistas, vacant except for more police, were transformed by the shift of scale and change of emphasis that so curiously affect a New York street when it is emptied of traffic.

The atmosphere of the city was exciting and portentous. You knew that not far away from you, men from all over the world were trying to find means to preserve their countries, their continents and their world, possibly even our planet. Then you reached the gallery, and there you found a bunch of artists playing at sticking string on paper and spraying it white, at covering the surface of a mirror with tacks, glued on head down, at cutting out crudely drawn paper dolls and hanging them from chicken wire, at ripping old nylon stockings and stretching them across odds and ends of wire or stuffing them with trash and tying the ends with string like nasty sausages. The air of the gallery seemed filled with little shrieks of perverse delight, and you were ashamed to be there and a part of it.

There are explanations and defenses for this kind of thing. They have been made thousands of times, but in the end each of them should be humiliating to the artist, although in his naïveté and self-love he has yet to realize it. The idea that this is an "art of protest" is most resounding, but it is also most specious, and the politest possible rebuttal is the single word, "baloney."

Back in 1916 we could legitimately say of dada—of which

the excesses among the exhibits at Martha Jackson's are coy and bloodless revivals—that its rejection of all reason and esthetics was a protest (of the cut-off-your-nose-to-spite-your-face kind) against a world that seemed to have gone mad or senile. But today, even if the world is still in a mess, men are trying as they have never tried before to find their way out of the mess. Negative social protest today is a form of cowardice, and to defend neo-dada at this moment as protest is to call the artists weak, foolish and vicious.

Another defense is the catch-all "art of our time." Let us pass this one by with the comment, obvious to anybody who visits the show, that here is an art created, to be sure, in our time, but by artists who by the bulk of the evidence on display are incapable of social responsibility, or unwilling to assume it, or ignorant of the fact that social responsibility devolves eventually upon the artist whether he wishes or not.

Then there is the point that this is all in good fun, only a divertissement—terribly amusing. Well, it isn't. The show is a repeat, with most of the same names represented, of the gallery's exhibition of last June. Nothing indicates the feebleness of its premise more than that in three months New Media—New Forms has become Stale Media—Stale Forms.

So where are we? We are left, as a matter of fact, with one serious and valid reason for such an exhibition, which is this:

In a century that has not incorporated the artist significantly into its scheme, and has glutted our eyes with billions of images through photography and through reproductions of painting (from billboards to the finest art books), the artist is left to scavenge for whatever means he can find to re-establish himself as a creator, to dissociate his product from the familiar images of the camera and the machine. His hope is to discover an anti-photographic and a mechanically unre-produceable technique of expression by experimenting with innumerable new media and new forms from which one, two, half a dozen, may prove serviceable.

Yet how pathetic this subterfuge is. And how incompetent, in this show, the artist seems as explorer. There are some artists here like Enrico Donati, whose concretions of color, pattern and texture have maintained for years a level of ornamental distinction; like Zoltan Kemeny, whose ingenuity is more than arresting. But it seems to me that they and the handful of others who have reached some solution to the problem would take one look at their neighbors and with-draw. For the company they keep here infers, somehow, that in spite of their achievement they have only gone farther than others toward the end of an impasse, not to mention that they are part of a sideshow in which an artist of imagi-nation and discretion is contaminated.

On its first go-round, "New Media—New Forms" was an engaging end-of-season circus. On its second, it is a disaster. It seems to me that anyone who visits it must abandon whatever interest he has in contemporary art or in collecting it, and spend his time brushing up on world affairs and his money on whatever cause might conceivably alleviate human suffering rather than encouraging human fatuity.

October 2, 1960

GARGOYLES FOR THE MACHINE AGE:
"Junk Sculpture" as Romantic Art.

Contemporary sculptors, who for some reason are about ten times as imaginative as contemporary painters, are having a wonderful time these days concocting a breed of monsters that can either scare the daylights out of you or tickle your ribs, depending on the nature of your sensibility to a form of art that combines wit with tentative forays into regions of darkness peculiar to the twentieth century. Although scrap metal is a favorite material of these sculptors, and the welding gun their most necessary tool, they have a lot in common with the medieval stone carvers whose cathedral gargoyles were the offspring of a similarly mixed but high-spirited marriage between the humorous and the sinister that produced its natural hybrid, the grotesque.

Fear of hell on one hand and rollicking gusto for life on the other produced the medieval gargoyles. Today we have ceased to believe in hell, and gusto is in short supply. But neo-gargoyle sculpture (the phrase is the invention of a colleague, Stuart Preston) can be interpreted as the expression of contemporary fears plus a contemporary zest for experiment and speculation.

A typical new gargoyle may be composed of such detritus of the machine age as discarded gears, pipes, metal meshes, screens and gratings, bits of iron or steel plate, and any of the thousands of discs, perforated plates, or oddly shaped and punctured units that have been stamped out to serve a

EDUARDO PAOLOZZI: *JASON*, 1956. 66″ high.
Bronze. Collection of the Museum of Modern Art,
New York.

special purpose yet become esthetic curiosa when accepted out of context as objects with an independent existence. Cinders and slag are good too, with their horrendous textures and bizarre shapes. Even the sculptors who work with new material like to gash it, melt it, score it, pit it, and crumple it into proper condition.

All art being a process of the transformation of material into expression, the term junk sculpture need be no more derogatory than the term oil painting. Junk sculpture becomes art when it meets the terms that make other forms of sculpture "good" or "bad" art. By one general definition, classical in implication, art is the distillation of order and meaning from the chaotic material of human experience. By direct analogy, if the junk sculptor can take the chaotic detritus of our machine age and reassemble it into forms that have a satisfactory relationship to one another as an esthetic whole, then he has indeed created a legitimate work of art from material—both physical and ideological— afforded only by our time.

The classical premises of purity and order, however, are dubious ones for the defense of junk sculpture. But turn the junk sculptor loose on romantic premises and he has it made. The job of the romantic is not to purify but to intensify, not to resolve but to stimulate, not so much to answer as to ask, and when he does answer, to answer by implication rather than by definition. Suggestion, free association, experiment, revolt, even fortuitous accident, are his meat. And the romantic artist has always had an interest in the exploration of decay that makes one wonder why it took him so long to discover the junk heap as his happiest hunting ground.

The fascination held by ruined machinery for the sculptor today may have its parallel once removed in the fascination held by ruined architecture for his nineteenth-century counterpart. His junk gargoyles suggest mangled and intermingled mutations of men, birds, beasts, and machines. His ruins are not reminders of the past, crumbling in the weather and devoured by foliage like the ones adored a hundred years ago, but are deformed as if prophetically by the aberrations of science that may yet produce the ultimate holocaust. This is the hell that we can conceive of today, and some of the gargoyles seem already to have approached close enough to its terrible boundaries to have been broken, seared, and fused into forms such as men have never seen, but might some day see too much of.

But of course it may not happen, and in the meanwhile man is up to an old trick of mental self-preservation: a large element of fun is introduced into fearful conjectures. This accounts for the double-barreled appeal of the new gargoyles. Things are pretty bad, they imply, and may get worse. But in the meanwhile this shaky crust we are walking on has an interesting bounce to it.

Horizon, March, 1961

PART THREE:
Notes on Some Painters

PLAYBOY OF THE NETHER WORLD:
The Tactics of Salvador Dali.

Salvador Dali is a great problem. He has painted some pictures for which "wonderful" is a proper description. But the extremity of the public personality he has presented, that of a clamorously ambitious and unabashedly opportunistic man; the absurdity of his pronouncements about himself and his art; his appalling syntheses of mawkish religiosity, sentimental sexuality and abnormal psychology; his maddening way of skidding back and forth across the line that divides slickness from technical brilliance—all of this makes one ready to throw the baby out with the bathwater. Yet it is a very curious thing about this painter that the only virtue that he absolutely cannot be denied is, antithetically, the virtue that lies at the basis of all homespun philosophies; he is an awfully hard worker. Publicly a grasshopper who has read Freud, privately he is surely as industrious as an ant.

If part of the critic's job is to throw his weight where it will help establish balance in an out-of-balance situation, then the only logical course of action in the case of Dali is to apply the silent treatment to this noisiest artist of our generation. On the other hand, truth is better served by pointing out some of Dali's limitations to members of that large section of the public who, conditioned by the curious devices of American advertising, have come to equate Dali's importance as an artist with the length of his mustache.

The best reason for withholding comment, however, would be that in 1944 the late George Orwell said so much about Dali in a 5,000-word essay called "Benefit of Clergy" that he leaves room only for a postscript on Dali's deterioration during the last sixteen years, and said it so well that any writer who calls attention to this obscure essay must suffer by comparison. Let us summarize some of Orwell's observations, and then add a postscript on Dali's subsequent development, or, more accurately, his subsequent attacks on the problem of arresting, holding, and perhaps meriting wide attention.

"Benefit of Clergy," first written as a review of Dali's autobiography, *The Secret Life of Salvador Dali,* appeared in this country in 1946 in an Orwell volume published by Reynal & Hitchcock, *Dickens, Dali and Others,* which sold a miserable 2,000 copies. So far as I can learn, it has not been reprinted. But the essay must be available somewhere and I feel that it should be made required reading as an antidote to such essays as a recent one by A. Reynolds Morse of the Reynolds-Morse Foundation, Inc., Cleveland, touting Dali—of all people—as the artist who will save modern art from—of all things—decadence.

Orwell's point, in discussing Dali and his public as a sociological phenomenon, is precisely that the cult of Dali by a moneyed class is a symptom of decadence in our society. He asks why, "if you throw dead donkeys at people, they throw money back." This is an important question, and not one likely to occur spontaneously to those people who circulate through Dali exhibitions with an air proper to pilgrims confronted by holy relics.

Dali's career as an artist, rather than as a public stuntsman, has been a succession of efforts to find a use for his extraordinary talent as a draftsman in an age when realism has stopped paying off. "Suppose," Orwell asks in his essay, "that you have nothing in you except your egoism and a dexterity that goes no higher than the elbow; suppose that your real gift is for a detailed, academic, representational

style of drawing, your real métier to be an illustrator of sci-
entific textbooks. How then do you become Napoleon?"
(Dali having written, "At seven I wanted to be Napoleon.
And my ambition has been growing steadily ever since.")

"There is always," Orwell continues, "one escape: into
wickedness. At five, throw a little boy off a bridge, strike an
old doctor across the face with a whip and break his spec-
tacles—or, at any rate, dream about doing such things.
Twenty years later, gouge the eyes out of dead donkeys with
a pair of scissors. Along those lines you can always feel
yourself original. And after all, it pays! It is much less dangerous than crime."

As a surrealist, making his first success, Dali found a happy
use for his "dexterity no higher than the elbow." It was
perfect for the rendering of Freudian visions involving the
naughtinesses that obsessed him, and he created during that
period such mesmerized and disturbing paintings as the
Museum of Modern Art's "Persistence of Memory" and Philadelphia's "Premonition of Civil War," in which a morbid personality fused vividly with a morbid social condition. But
as surrealism waned (and, probably not coincidentally, as
the press became surfeited with his stunts), Dali tried to put
his miraculous forearm into the service of the one thing that
has always had a sure-fire audience, religion, and another
that had become a new god, science. He even combined the
two in "nuclear religious" paintings. At this point our postscript to Orwell's essay begins.

At this point also, Dali as an artist, even by synthesis,
began floundering. The "scientific" works are by the most
generous interpretation the result of a sincere struggle on
the part of an artist who, in middle age (Dali is fifty-six),
recognizes his emptiness and makes an effort to fill it with

something important to the very existence of the world. In this effort he may have reached the closest point to his "real métier as an illustrator of scientific textbooks," but these paintings are to the scientific spirit and achievements what space fiction is to Cape Canaveral.

As for the religious paintings: I suppose that no man has the right to say of another that his stated conversion to religion is an opportunistic pose. But certainly one has the right to say what one thinks when faced by Dali's intrusive and embarrassing holy pictures, the Crucifixion in the Metropolitan Museum and the Last Supper in the National Gallery in Washington. They seem to me to be blatant expressions of morbid eroticism, in which the artist has abused the right of sanctuary to the point of sacrilege. They are super-surrealist, filled with inner cancers rather than displaying the—in its way—honest rottenness that led Orwell to say of earlier Dalis, "They are diseased and disgusting, and any investigation ought to start out from that fact."

Let us pause to point out that not Orwell, nor anybody, denies Dali's right to paint what he pleases. And "Dali is a draftsman of very exceptional gifts. He is also, to judge by the minuteness and the sureness of his drawings, a very hard worker. He is an exhibitionist and a careerist, but he is not a fraud. He has fifty times more talent than most of the people who would denounce his morals and jeer at his paintings."

This is still true of Dali, but his exhibitionism is now sugar-coated by a synthetic goodness, truth and beauty, while his careerism is camouflaged by pseudo-intellectualism. In his recent work he has seized upon everything that has happened since he emerged with surrealism, as well as plenty that happened before. Never one to circumscribe

Salvador Dali: *HYPERXIOLOGICAL LANDSCAPE*, 1960-61. 12⅜″ x 17⅛″. Oil on canvas. Permission of the artist. Photograph courtesy Carstairs Gallery, New York.

himself, Dali has set out to summarize his century with the help of those preceding it.

Drawing from every source of current abstract art and experimental media but holding to his faith in detailed visual reality, he is trying—simply—to integrate everything that everyone is doing at the moment with everything that he has done so far. He points out that passages of rocks in "The Ecumenical Council," a hugely complicated picture upon which I would rather make no further comment, are painted in such a way that they are complete as abstract compositions yet serve at the same time as representational symbols. This is a reverse switch on the current amusement of taking

representational pictures and finding that sections may be
enlarged into abstractions. Dali works in this direction, too,
making studies of Fortuny, the nineteenth-century Spanish
academician, in a generally abstract expressionist manner.

He is following also the mode of "painting" with actual
objects, but with a variation. He introduces some human
teeth (gilded) and some real nails into a small painting,
"Hyperpsychological Heaven," and paints matching nails
illusionistically alongside. In the same picture he builds up
gobbets and drips of pigment, which merge with painted
drips, much in the way three-dimensional stage scenery may
merge with a painted backdrop that continues it in perspective. And, fascinated by Velasquez, Dali, like Picasso,
is doing variations on "Las Meniñas."

One thing is certain: The effort toward universal synthesis is sincere. But the question, in its least kind form, is
whether this synthesis has gone beyond the point of an
extreme eclecticism and even whether a certain amount of
poaching is not involved. You may look at the new Dalis in
one of two ways: sympathetically, as the most demanding
effort at universal assimilation made by any twentieth-century painter, or unsympathetically, as products of an avidity
similar to that of a greedy child who wants all the presents
under the Christmas tree for himself.

In the meanwhile, Dali remains a phenomenon, self-in-
vented if you wish, but a phenomenon for all that. The
final judgment on the Dali that Orwell wrote about may be
that he was a great talent corrupted and devoured by a sick-
ness that forced him to impersonate a clown, and on the
later Dali that his effort to cure himself left him only half
an artist. Wickedness was, as Orwell perceived, Dali's only

certain escape from mediocrity. He had a flair for it, and has been unable to find an effective substitute.

May 29 and December 4, 1960

LOPLOP THE WATERWITCH:
An Aspect of Max Ernst.

Max Ernst is an artist who gives the impression of having been diverted from a profession for which he was born—that of biologist, or of optometrist, or of wandering minstrel—by a hobby that took over his life.

As a painter, Ernst offers evidence of only a moderate degree of natural talent: that is, he is not manually dexterous. He can't draw (or at least he doesn't draw) in the sense of the draftsman who records the structure and character of an object by whatever means. He seems barely able to represent a rubbery, jointed cylinder in such a way that it is identifiable as an arm. He is better at cutting and pasting, and he can combine photoengravings of (for instance) an old biplane, a swan, a mirror, and three heads of cherubs in a way that alters the trite and rational into the bizarre and disturbing. With such concoctions he can produce an uneasy laughter similar to that inspired by today's "sick comics," although his surface is more whimsical than mordant.

Ernst's collages and alterations of this kind were part of the dada movement through which he found himself as an artist—not through its impertinence and nihilism but through its discovery that familiar things thrown out of kilter may serve as divining rods for the discovery of the supernatural. At 70 Ernst remains a dependable waterwitch; his forked stick detects spring after spring of magic. Sometimes the flow is only a trickle, but it is pure, and he is in contrast with some of his fellow sorcerers, like Dali, who used to be able to produce a torrent but have lately been striking a series of dry holes.

For the catalogue of his retrospective exhibition at the Museum of Modern Art, Ernst supplied "An Informal Life of M. E.," in which he recalls that in 1891 "On the second of April at 9:45 A.M. Max Ernst hatched from the egg which his mother had laid in an eagle's nest and over which the bird had brooded for seven years."

Taking this at face value, we read on to the year 1906, when Ernst was going on 15: "First contact with the occult, magic and witchcraft: On the night of the fifth of January one of his closest friends, a most intelligent and affectionate pink cockatoo, died. It was a terrible shock to Max when, in the morning, he discovered the dead body and when, at the same moment, the father announced the birth of a sister.

"In his imagination Max coupled these two events and charged the baby with the extinction of the bird's life. There followed a series of mystical crises, fits of hysteria, exaltations and depressions. A dangerous confusion between birds and humans became fixed in his mind and asserted itself in his drawings and paintings. (Later M. E. identified himself voluntarily with Loplop, Bird Superior.)"

The tone of this memoir, which should appeal equally to admirers of A. A. Milne and students of abnormal psychology, is echoed visually in Ernst's picturizations of Loplop, who may combine the engaging ingenuousness of

Donald Duck with the eeriness of an ectoplasmic manifestation. It seems impossible to think of Ernst except in terms of syntheses, hybridization of opposites, and grafting, although one never thinks of him as eclectic. He has been industrious, inventive and personal in assembling his artistic vocabulary from a variety of unexpected sources, and his conceptions are never less than artful.

A single picture—for instance, "The Eye of Silence," a complicated fantastic landscape in which Ernst forces to the limit his talent for ingenious technical devices—may declare its descent from an oddly mixed marriage between early nineteenth-century German romantic landscape and a medical textbook on cysts and blastulas, with family recessives popping up in forms suggestive of paleontology, minerology, art nouveau, Albrecht Altdorfer and possibly Gustave Doré. Compounded of so many elements, a picture should be a mess, but "The Eye of Silence" is beautifully assembled and its multiple components lose their separate identities and fuse into pure Ernst.

Because he feeds upon so many sources and makes the single contribution of amalgamation for his own pleasure, Ernst seems to me to be a sport from a contemporary type, the spectator intellectual in the twentieth century. In an age when research in every field, including the nature of the past and the probable nature of the future, has built a structure of knowledge so vast and so complex that no single man can begin to understand it all, the intellectual is a specialist within a narrow field or a spectator of the whole in so far as he can stretch his horizon.

In science especially we expect to understand only the slightest fraction of theory or of practice, but we are fascinated by all its tangible expressions. Again and again and again Ernst is attracted to the graphic forms of scientific illustration, but only as phenomena unrelated to their function. The colophon of his retrospective is a graph lifted intact and without credit from Jahnke and Emde's "Tables of Functions," to which the artist has done nothing except add his name by blackening a sequence of graph squares. Thus a diagram that demonstrated something called "The Bessel function $Jp(x)$ of the two real variables x and p" becomes identified with the artist simply because he liked the look of it as an independent pattern and used it ingeniously for his own ends.

Whether or not Ernst has overstepped any limits in such obvious borrowing (as the person thinks who called the source of the colophon to my attention) is not much of a point. But in a very direct way the use of a scientific diagram in a personal and entirely unscientific way typifies at its extreme the response of the individual to the externals of a system of knowledge upon which our civilization is based but which none of us except a few scientists can understand.

In using material of this kind and material borrowed from other sciences—sometimes as directly as this and sometimes in fantastic concoctions that give it double pictorial meanings—Ernst is using for the ends of personal expression the kind of thing that other spectator intellectuals amuse themselves by watching. An artist of paradox, he paradoxically transforms the logic of science into the illogic of magic. The scientist's laboratory supplies the witch's cauldron not with eye of newt and toe of frog, wool of bat and tongue of dog, —but with Bessel functions, molecular structures, microphotographs and innumerable other visual expressions of an invisible world.

March 5, 1961

THE DELIGHTFUL DISCONCERTER:
René Magritte.

René Magritte is a Belgian artist who, at 64, is a contender for the title of the leading fantasist painter today. By classification Magritte is a surrealist, and he participated in the union of horseplay and intellectualism that established surrealism as his century's version of man's spottily continuous exploration of the world of dream and necromancy. But even as an official surrealist, Magritte has always remained a little outside the movement, or any other movement, in a way that is refreshing.

The fact that the word "refreshing" can be used in connection with him is the first indication of the difference between Magritte and his colleagues. His power as a fantasist is not so much that he presents us with the fantastic as something unexplainable, as that he presents it to us as something unquestioned. A fantasist of Dali's ilk offers us a conglomeration of impossibilities that partially convince simply because they are presented in acute detail. Dali takes us into madhouses where we remain sane observers or, say, to a cocktail party of freaks where our normalcy may make us feel out of place but leads us to no questioning of that normalcy as the standard from which the rest of the company departs.

But Magritte takes us to a party where all the guests are normal but one. This one is a person who, while perfectly natural in every other way, floats around the ceiling like an escaped balloon. This floating, however, seems to be taken for granted; the other guests obviously accept it as nothing extraordinary; to point out the abnormality would be rude at best and dangerous at worst, since we begin to wonder why we, alone, find the circumstance unusual. The end is that we begin not to doubt our own eyes but to doubt our experience that has taught us that people do not float. We are taken into the world of the fantastic as a participant, rather than as a spectator. By his matter-of-factness and by a kind of pictorial understatement—an economy in the use of fantastic elements combined with commonplace ones—Magritte seduces us into the act, while Dali merely performs for us as we watch.

Magritte contrasts also with another Belgian of his generation, Paul Delvaux. Much closer to the surreal norm, Delvaux is conspicuously engaged in the Freudian, semi-Freudian, or pseudo-Freudian sexualities that are uppermost in the public personality of the movement. Not that Magritte has not turned out some jobs of this kind—and some startling ones—but he has tended to work away from rather than deeper into such themes. Delvaux on the other hand is a painter so sexual as to be embarrassing upon occasion. His nudes, although young and of proportions that should be adequately attractive, have the anti-allure of individuals stripped for medical attention and probably in need of it.

Magritte's fantasies can be subjected to psychoanalytical inspection, since there is almost nothing that cannot be, even when fantasy is not involved. A picture called "Night at Pisa," for instance, involves a tower and a spoon of the same height, propping one another up. It supplies pat elementary symbols for any amateur psychiatrist. But to play this game with Magritte is to make mere charades, essentially literary charades, of paintings that have admirably little dependence

René Magritte: *LE CHÂTEAU DES PYRÉNÉES*, 1955-59. 78⅝″ x 55⅛″. Oil on canvas. Collection of Harry Torczyner, New York.

upon literary associations. The trouble with much surrealism is that it goes over the edge that divides the art of painting from the art of literature—becomes, in short, illustration, thus losing its independence as a purely visual art. Magritte usually avoids this error, although he takes us out of this world into an eerie one just as a teller of fantastic tales may do.

But he takes us out of this world not by narrating an incident but by dissolving the concepts of time and space and volume and tangible relatives upon which our experience of this world is based. "Night at Pisa" sounds explicit enough, and an explicit list could be made of the elements that compose it. But it is totally unexplicit on the scores that attach us to this world and account for whatever security we may feel within it. Is the tower normal sized and the spoon huge, or the spoon normal and the tower dwarfed? More than being either, they are neither. We do not really know what the size of things is, and as a result we do not really know what size we are. The sensation of lost scale must be akin to that of weightlessness experienced by an astronaut; within a Magritte we are as far removed from this world as is the man in the space ship.

Magritte's manipulation of scale is his most explicable device, although the subtleties of his control remain unaccountable, just as we can point out but not entirely explain the effectiveness of his denial of materiality when he gives one substance, a rock, the property of another, a gas, by making it a weightless object in mid-air. And in any case these elements in Magritte's art, basic as they are, are shared by other surrealists.

What separates Magritte, in the end, from other surrealists is that the pretentious morbidities upon which the school has too often fed, and which finally become so wearisome, have never dominated his themes and have flavored them less and less in his late work. Never pretentious, Magritte is sometimes content to be merely delightfully witty, as in "The Plagiarism," where a spring landscape with blossoming trees is revealed through an illusionistic cut-out shape recognizable as a bouquet of flowers.

Historically, other artists have had more to do with the development of surrealism and modern fantasy than has Magritte. Max Ernst is one of these. But Ernst is as much a pictorial littérateur as he is a painter; and as a painter he is as much a fabricator of abstract patterns as he is a creator of fantasies. Magritte, on the other hand, is a painter of absolutely concrete impossibilities that tell no story. His genius is that he enchants the eye as an entrance to the mind, which he equally delights and disconcerts.

Horizon, January, 1962
(abridged)

MAN BARKING AT THE MOON:
Joan Miró at Work and Play.

Joan Miró, an artist to whom the uninitiated sometimes refer as "she," to their subsequent embarrassment, is a male Spaniard who was born in Catalonia in 1893, and his first name is nothing more esoteric than the Catalan version of Juan. He lives and works nowadays almost exclusively in Majorca, near his married daughter and his two grandchildren, although he makes an occasional foray back to Paris, where as a young painter he began the classical gamut from near-starvation to participation in esthetic revolts to gradual recognition, and then to fame and fortune. But people who remember him from his early days recall that he was always something of an outlander among his contemporaries—neat, precise and detached on the sidelines of gatherings that tended toward Bohemian display and general ruckus.

Today, in his sixties, Miró is a short, sturdy, quiet man with a round head and a square face which, with its large, poetic dark eyes, its potato nose and its sad mouth, somehow suggests that of a clown out of make-up. The colors of his pictures—pure reds, yellows and blues, bright greens, oranges and violets, set off by snowy whites and sooty black lines and patches—are circus colors. Their gaiety is the gaiety of the clown's painted mouth and the forms they describe are rollicking, humorous ones. But, as everyone knows, the clown is an informal philosopher beneath the paint. So is Miró.

Being a modern artist not only by the definition of "modern" to be found in the dictionary, but also by the one to be found on the lips of the vulgar as an artist who paints "that crazy stuff my 6-year-old kid could do better than," Miró has naturally found passionate attackers and passionate defenders. Nowadays his prices, also, are passionate, and he is in the happy position of being able to ignore both attackers and defenders and to paint as he pleases.

But this, in truth, he has always done ("Painting is made as we make love, a total embrace, prudence thrown to the wind, nothing held back"), even when he was too obscure to be either attacked or defended, and so poor that hallucinations produced by hunger supplied him with subjects for some of his most eerie canvases. We have his own word as to

JOAN MIRÓ: *FEMMES, OISEAU, ÉTOILES*, 1942. 42½″ x 23⅜″. Pencil and pastel. Courtesy Pierre Matisse Gallery, New York.

this source of inspiration. His description of those times as "pretty hard" is substantiated by the diet they enforced: one lunch a week, with dried figs and chewing gum the other six days.

During those years, the early nineteen twenties, you could have bought a modest Miró for a few hundred francs, and an important one for a few hundred dollars at the most. Today, his "Dog Barking at the Moon," showing a piebald pup, a moon affected by some kind of tumorous disorder, a wavering horizon, and a ladder inexplicably balanced at an angle and yearning toward the zenith like an upended railroad track, would cost you $25,000 if it were for sale at its insured value—which it is not—and it would probably bring a multiple of that figure if it were put up at auction before our best-heeled collectors.

In the early twenties Ernest Hemingway, an impoverished but hopeful journalist, shot dice with a friend for the privilege of buying Miró's "The Farm" for 5,000 francs (about $200), paying for it on the installment plan, since $30 had been his ceiling offer for pictures up until then. ("When I first knew Miró he had very little money and very little to eat and he worked all day every day for nine months painting a very large and wonderful picture called 'The Farm.'") Today "The Farm" is worth, unofficially, about $100,000. A little simple arithmetic indicates that this is a 49,900 per cent increase.

Confronted with this most generally respected yardstick of merit, creating an identification between Miró and I.B.M. stock, the average person's first question is a stunned, sincere, puzzled "Why?" There are several reasons, four of which are listed here in ascending order of validity:

(1) Snob value. This affects prices, but otherwise may be

dismissed as impertinent, or at best a matter to be discussed by sociologists.

(2) Skillful handling by dealers expert in the care and feeding of reputations. This, too, we may shelve as being true for successful bad painters as well as for successful good painters, of honest dealers and of charlatans equally.

Tied for most important place:

(3) The existence of numbers of people with that kind of money to spend, who get that much pleasure out of owning a Miró and having it on hand to look at.

(4) The fact that, over the decades, critics who should know have come more and more to regard Miró as the most important post-cubist artist. If they are right, this means that the three great names in the revolution that has transformed art in our half-century are Matisse (fauvism), Picasso (cubism) and Miró. Thus, "Dog Barking at the Moon" and "The Farm," as key pictures in Miró's development, are possessed of that combination of historical and esthetic significance that leads collectors and museum directors to fracture the Tenth Commandment, which has to do with not coveting. Add to this the fact that since both pictures are of types that Miró no longer produces, they already have the kind of rarity value that jumps the prices of an important artist's work after his death.

Prices aside, why is Miró so important? This is difficult to explain without summarizing the development of contemporary painting, but in a crowded nutshell it would go something like this:

Miró, in working through the successive stages of his own development, has had the experience of conventional academic training, has absorbed the revolutionary color theory of fauvism (too complicated to discuss here), has experimented with the structural fissions and reunions of cubism (even more complicated), and has been a leader in that wild mixture of nonsense, showmanship, compulsive insolence, and serious experiment which was first "dada" and then surrealism, the cult of the rational-irrational.

From all of these he has kept what has suited him as an intensely personal artist. In a world more and more given over to practical and scientific values, he has affirmed the legitimacy of the magical, the poetic, the lyrical. He has kept open for us the door to a world we have almost forgotten, the world of myth and the supernatural, a world sometimes joyous, sometimes monstrous, grotesque, ludicrous, sometimes lovely, sometimes terrifying, but always fascinating because it is rooted in the earliest consciousness of man.

That is a large statement, but it can be defended:

The standard criticism leveled against "modern" painters, including Miró, is that they have sacrificed centuries of tradition in order to create their little sensations. But Miró is the contemporary master of a tradition that goes back, say, some 30,000 years—a tradition in which the distinction between philosophy and voodoo may become a matter of semantics, but one that begins with the first works of art created by primitive man—magical symbols scratched in rock to exorcise demons or to placate the forces of nature.

A picture by Miró may be as simple (or may appear to be) and as disturbing as these. The monstrous little creatures he concocts are the kind of sorcerer's images that would scare the bearskin off a neolithic man if he should return to his cave to find them scratched on his wall, or would reassure him when he turned in for the night if he had scratched them there himself as his guardians against evil spirits.

Children take this kind of picture in their stride, accepting Miró's hieroglyphic fantasies as easily as they accept the illustrations of gnomes and dwarfs in their story books, but their parents, occupying a middle ground between innocence and philosophical speculation, are left puzzled or infuriated.

If they turn to books on Miró for help, they are likely to be left glassy-eyed by a writer who states that "the main impact of the image comes from an autonomous caricatural energy and from a precise balance of biomorphic forms." This is a remarkably succinct summary and it makes sense as a capsule analysis applicable to dozens of Mirós, but it is not for everybody.

Also, Miró's own statement that he wants the ideas in his pictures to "give the spectator an immediate blow between the eyes before a second thought can interpose" is likely to make people draw back a little. Even if they get the blow, they don't always get the idea. Except as an investment by hindsight, not many members of the general public would buy a Miró even if it could still be picked up for loose change.

This is too bad, for Miró is not difficult to understand, which means to enjoy. But he will never mean anything much to anybody who cannot accept the premise that the prankish surface of his art, like the surface of great clowning, may be scratched to reveal meanings that are serious to one degree or another. The situation is complicated by the hazard that the scratch may widen into a chasm from whose bottom the smoke of brimstone rises, illuminated by glow of hellfire.

Miró's basic assumption is that wit and nightmare not only may coexist in a picture but may be indistinguishable from one another. He is the wittiest artist painting today, but as often as not he uses his wit as a kind of flashlight to investigate the darkest areas of a subterranean, a primeval, a tor-

mented and sinister world, a modern Hades where the shade
of Freud occupies the throne formerly held by Pluto, and
the disturbed subconscious has replaced what we used to
call, in days innocent almost beyond memory, the soul.

The joy of Miró—for he is a delightful painter—is that he
shows us that morbidity may involve humor, that the maca-
bre may draw sustenance from the comical, that nightmare
and hallucination may be compatible with high style. Words-
worth's idea that poetry is emotion recollected in tranquillity
might be applied to Miró as a poetic painter, which he is; in
Miró, the recollection of the insane agony of night, recalled
the morning after, is downright fun.

His painted shapes float and dance, leer and sleep, rise and
sink, swell, stiffen, or relax, join and divide, repeat, echo or
contradict one another, on canvases which may be enjoyed at one level in the nursery, and at another in the
psychiatric ward. Nevertheless, these canvases find their
proper and important place in the history of art as the end
result—so far—of the tradition of fantasy that can be followed from the caves on into ancient Greece with its centaurs
and Cyclopes and other monsters, into the Middle Ages with
their gargoyles and hellscapes, and then into our own time
with Miró, after centuries during which the tradition was
running thin.

Humor is usually a part of fantasy, but laughter is especially a part of Miró's art. It is not always happy laughter.
People have been known to laugh from shock, and they often
laugh because, finding themselves suddenly in some threatening and inexplicable circumstance, they don't know what
else to do. Many a painting by Miró can be well enough
defined as a threatening and inexplicable circumstance, and
may stimulate laughter of a kind unconnected with anything

having to do with, for instance, the drolleries of Bob Hope or Jerry Lewis.

Such a point is made of Miró's wit—here and elsewhere whenever he is written about—that in spite of premonitions of defeat this might be the place to attempt an explanation for any reader who does not find wit in Miró's pictures but has been dogged enough to follow this article thus far in hope of illumination. With a firm grasp on our bootstraps, and with the dictionary open in front of us, we may be able to hurdle the distinction between verbal wit, with which we are familiar, and pictorial wit, which is at least analogous.

The most helpful phrase in the dictionary's definition is "ingenious contrivance," which certainly is a Miró to a T. And how about "cleverly apt expression of connections between ideas which awaken amusement"? For the Miró lover, each form or line is clever and apt, and an expression of an idea or a combination of ideas, sometimes apparent, sometimes slyly hidden, sometimes a little perverse, but always present in a juxtaposition that awakens amusement. Yet there is not much to be done to relieve the bafflement of the person who says, honestly and in frustration, that he finds no ideas in Miró, or no connection between any he can find, and that in any case he—deadly phrase—is not amused.

Miró's compatriot, Picasso, asked to explain the meaning of one of his pictures, once said that if he could have said in words what he wanted to say, he would have written a book, not painted a picture. Perhaps the thing to do is to admit that Miró, like caviar, is not for the rank and file. But it is likely that anyone who experiments with gastronomy will develop a taste for caviar, and that anyone who investigates the world of painting will eventually find pleasure in Miró.

He is, after all, so personal an artist that he says most to those observers whose reaction to a picture finally boils down, quite simply, to the question of whether or not they enjoy it, all theorizing and verbalizing and examination of reasons aside.

Miró's essential intimacy explains why his pictures do not infuriate for long even the antagonists of modern art. Against Picasso, the grievances of the unsympathetic have a way of increasing in virulence upon longer acquaintance; with Miró they are more likely to simmer down, modified by a recognition that if he wants to paint like that, it's his own business. This is exactly Miró's attitude, which should settle the matter for everyone.

March 15, 1959

THE PERFECT DUET:
Calder and Miró, an Exhibition Review.

Occasionally a play, a movie, a musical performance or an art exhibition comes along that is just about perfect, and that is a happy day for the critic. The Perls Galleries last week supplied such an occasion by juxtaposing thirteen mobiles by Alexander Calder and thirteen paintings by Joan Miró in what must be the happiest exhibition of the season. It could easily carry the title "The Joy of Living," since it is bright, fresh and vigorous, or with equal appropriateness "The Joy of Doing," since these two artists relay to the observer a tremendous gusto in the disciplined creative act.

ALEXANDER CALDER: *WIDOW*, 1952. 7′ high. Standing mobile. Courtesy of the artist.

And for any visitor the exhibition must be an experience in the joy of seeing.

Both Calder and Miró have the capacity for lightheartedness without superficiality. They are wits, but never gagmen. Among the most original artists alive, with two of the most sharply individualized styles to be found anywhere, they manage to create prolifically and yet to avoid the pitfalls of the prolific stylist—repetition and monotony. They are inventors extraordinary, contrivers of the bizarre but not peddlers of novelty. Their zest, perkiness and humor can delight a child who asks of a Calder only that it be a fascinating gadget, of a Miró only that it picture hobgoblins and quaint creatures in vivid colors.

At this obvious level Calder and Miró are delectable enough for anybody. But beyond it, Calder's turning, hovering and floating shapes are spatial designs of a precision that can be called classical, and Miró's fantasies are a communion with the world of magic incantation that inspired the first works of art produced by men but is accessible today only to the most exquisitely civilized talents.

Such talents enter that world not through the cultivation of naïveté (a contradiction in terms and a bad mistake in reasoning that can produce only lisping pseudo-primitive trash) but through what the late Francis Henry Taylor, speaking of Paul Klee, once called, in conversation, "a fourth-dimensional innocence."

This irreplaceable phrase, which I will continue to borrow until somebody points out that I have worn it threadbare, distinguishes better than most book-length discussions could distinguish between retrogression to elementary mentality and the artful use of elementary forms in the service of complicated expression. Calder has shown that the construction toy can be the seed of an abstract demonstration that remains enchanting as an object, all analytical pleasures aside; while Miró has shown that the most obvious scrawls of savages and children may be adapted in a post-Freudian society to abash and delight us by their half-caricatural revelation of the primitive rites that, in disguise, continue to make life worth living in the drawing room.

As a craftsman, Calder has the directness and the careful assurance of an expert machinist. He is the kind of workman you wish you could find in your garage, but never do. Alongside him his imitators are bunglers and their work appears to have been assembled from kits that came with a faulty set of directions. His sturdy metal constructions often seem to have grown as logically and as beautifully as ferns and may have the same supple delicacy.

But even when his mobiles bear such titles as "Black Scorpion," "Red Flowers," or "Monkey Tail," descriptive associations are of little importance in Calder's work. A difference between him and Miró is that if Calder had to be straitjacketed into an unqualified category we would have to call him an artist of pure form, while Miró would be one of romantic impulse. But their degree of common ground is emphasized in their happy combination here—the element of fantasy is heightened in Calder's impeccably balanced structures and the element of calculation becomes more apparent than usual in Miró's looser inventions. For me, the juxtaposition resulted more in a new way of seeing Miró through Calder than the other way around. Miró's hitherto flat patterns became legible in a variety of planes, with lines and circles translating themselves—whether they should have or not—into Calderish wires and discs.

Actually, the Mirós, although they range across a period of thirty years, seem to have been selected for their special affinities with the Calders (which range over ten). The affinities are close, shape by shape as well as beneath the surface, where the essential character of a work of art resides. This character is vivacious, even playful. But in works of a kind not represented here, Miró can lead you, in what seems to be a game, to the edges of sinister places. He can open an abyss just beyond your toes, can lift the humorous disguise for a moment from a monster who is not at all benign.

This difference from Calder is not hinted at in the present show, and although its absence accounts for the show's remarkable unity, it might also leave Miró a bit less of an artist than he really is, at least for anyone who expects to find in the thirteen paintings anything like a complete summary of Miró's statement. But if this is not Miró at his most profound, it is Miró at his most entrancing. And he also turns up as a poet in words as well as in paint, since the exhibition's catalogue reproduces the holograph of a few lines dedicated to his friend Calder.

Calder in turn has contributed a brief statement of his first meeting and early acquaintance with Miró. The friendship, of thirty years' standing, is projected from every part of the two small rooms so happily filled, and completes the distinction of this extraordinary show.

February 26, 1961

NATURAL WONDER:
Andrew Wyeth and "Our Time."

Andrew Wyeth's art denies the values of modernism, yet he is collected by museums and individuals dedicated to contemporary standards. Technically he is an acute realist, yet his art is subjective, poetic, even lyrical. He belongs to no school, yet he is firmly a part of a native American tradition. He paints entirely to please himself, yet he comes as close as any painter today to pleasing everybody. He has never directed his art toward a market, least of all the present market, yet some twenty collectors are in queue for first chance at any picture that comes from his studio.

Wyeth's subject-matter is homely, yet the end effect of his pictures is bewitchment. If it were absolutely necessary to classify him within one of the major isms that have dominated twentieth-century painting—fauvism and expressionism, cubism and geometrical abstraction, surrealism and fantasy—he would have to be grouped with the surrealists, in a grotesque union of opposites. He shares with surrealists the use of precisely detailed imagery as the vocabulary of visionary statement. But where surrealist imagery is morbid, exotic or fanciful, Wyeth's is healthy, familiar and natural.

The price of $35,000 paid by the Philadelphia Museum of Art for Wyeth's "Ground Hog Day" established a record as the highest ever paid outright by a museum for a painting by an American during his lifetime. But a high sales price, especially for a contemporary painting, may be the result of week-end excitement, and in any case is no dependable gauge of esthetic merit. Like the price of any other marketable commodity today, a painting's price is only an index of supply and demand, and this market, like any other, can be rigged. Supply can be arbitrarily controlled and demand can be artificially stimulated.

In Wyeth's case, the controls are natural. Supply is limited by his slow production (he is not only a meticulous painter, but also one for whom each painting is an experience in growth through reflection) and demand has grown of itself.

ANDREW WYETH: *GROUND HOG DAY*, 1959. 31″ x 31¾″. Tempera on panel. Collection of the Philadelphia Museum of Art. Photograph by A. J. Wyatt, Staff Photographer.

This combination of circumstances is exceptional enough, but what is most exceptional is that while Wyeth obviously offers people something that they ardently desire in painting, he has remained a one-man school. Where are the sincere followers at best, the opportunistic imitators at worst, whom we would expect to find respectively echoing the ideas and tapping the market of a painter who has demonstrated the richness of both?

An explanation is that Wyeth is not what is called a painter "of our time," that viciously limiting phrase thrown about to characterize gaudy hit-and-run experiments and serious ones also, but based always on the premise that the present has nothing to do with the past. Wyeth is concerned with values no more peculiar to our time than to any other—timeless ones, in short, which he approaches in an extremely personal way. By a final paradox, he is a conspicuously "different" painter, without ever having cultivated differentness, in a time when differentness is a painter's fetish.

To judge from what he has said about the conceptions of his paintings, Wyeth draws more heavily than from any other source on recollections of boyhood and adolescence, but he reflects upon these as a grown man free from nostalgia for lost innocence, and preoccupied with finding the deepest sources of human feeling that account for our earliest, most spontaneous emotional experience of nature. His early work was a semi-illustrationistic celebration of the look of nature; his more mature pictures have been intensely sympathetic investigations of the solitary identities of human beings, usually simple ones, within the framework of nature.

He has steadily pared away from his subject matter all accessory elements that could make possible its confusion with genre painting (a level at which many of his admirers will continue to accept him, and his few detractors continue to reject him). In "Ground Hog Day" and another recent work now in a private collection, "River Cove," he includes no figures, and achieves a further penetration into nature where the artist observes as if magically disembodied.

"Ground Hog Day" shows a portion of a room where a single cup and saucer are set on a table by a window through which we see a portion of a country yard in the pale sunlight of late winter or early spring. "River Cove" shows a bit of sandy bank with a scattering of pebbles and shells sloping down into clear water that reflects, in the upper quarter of the composition, a band of otherwise unseen trees. A few heron tracks suggest that we see the cove as an alighting heron might do. The picture is filled with light and air (as is "Ground Hog Day"), but a kind of light and air opposed to the impressionist idea of prismatic vibrations obscuring the details of form. The light is of extraordinary purity without heightened brilliance, and the air, instead of softening objects as they recede, is like an all-encompassing lens by which the eye sees with miraculous clarity every diminutive element that goes into the formation of every object, large or small.

Such precisely detailed description of the minutiae of nature is the most obvious element in the world Wyeth is now creating. But in itself, of course, it has about the same expressive value as the Lord's Prayer engraved on the head of a pin. To this extent Wyeth has his equals among a few painters who labor their surfaces with microscopic details, but the artistry that combines Wyeth's details into an expressive unit is beyond them. For all its complication square inch by square inch, "River Cove" has the overall simplicity, subtle and harmonious, of a Chinese wash drawing. Such a picture can be created only by a man with a special and meaningful response to the world as well as a technical capacity equal and appropriate to its crystallization in paint.

This is a rare combination and is reason enough for Wyeth's isolation. But there are other first-rate artists than Wyeth around, and they have been impelled to paint in antithetical manners. The explanation must be that in a time when speed, flash and immediate impact rule so much of our lives, they must also rule most painters' ways of expression.

But not Wyeth's. Through whatever circumstances, his world is one of poetic contemplation in a time dominated by erratic sensation.

October 11, 1959

ROUND TRIP:

Charles Burchfield's Journey of Exploration.

A lot has happened to American art during the near half-century of Charles Burchfield's career. This year he is 68, but his new paintings are very close to the Burchfields dated 1916, when he was a sprouting 23 and was given his first exhibition.

Say that about most painters and you would be describing a man who, having found a successful formula, has devoted himself to repeating it, commercializing it and desiccating it. Not Mr. Burchfield.

The new paintings are fantasies, and so were those of 1916. But they are a return to fantasy, without equivocation, after years of preoccupation with the American scene in its industrial, urban and semi-rural aspects of a man-botched countryside, and more years during which Burchfield has been working his way back to fantasy, often with discouraging indications that he might be losing his way. Now that he has come full circle, it is apparent that he knew where he was going and has learned a lot during the trip.

The sun, the moon and the turn of the seasons in a world of nature where joyousness and violence are never far apart are the theme of Burchfield's newest paintings. These are not exactly landscapes; they are no closer to topography than they are to weather reports. Although they use the forms of nature—everything from flowers to planets—as points of departure, they are mystical explorations of a world essentially primeval. The existence of man is not recognized in them, except as a spirit whose observation of the annual cycle of growth, rest and rebirth gives meaning to phenomena.

Actually, the phenomena of nature have been the persistent meaningful factor in all of Burchfield's work, even when he seemed to depart furthest from the natural world into the man-made one. The Fine Arts Gallery of San Diego owns a Burchfield, "Rainy Night," of 1930, which is all pavement, brick and metal. There is not a plant or a spot of earth visible in this cityscape of two intersecting streets and their ugly buildings backed up by water tanks. But the undefeatable sky and the rain that falls everywhere transforming dirty asphalt into a reflector like a lake, are what the picture is really about. Pictures of this kind established Burchfield as a major American painter, a position that is certainly deserved, but half of the time these pictures were only half understood by the people who admired them.

Burchfield is always thought of as two painters, first the poet of the early fantasies and then the "socially conscious" painter connected with regionalism and the re-discovery of the American scene. This is a mistaken idea, for he has consistently been a poet and a very personal kind of poet, even though his two kinds of poetry are not compatible and have resulted in some bad garbles when he has tried to mesh them in a single picture.

CHARLES BURCHFIELD: *WINTER TWILIGHT*, 1930. 27¾″ x 30½″. Oil on composition board. Collection of the Whitney Museum of American Art, New York.

With social consciousness and realism in bad favor with painters and critics today, Burchfield's return to pure fantasy will be welcomed as a return to the right road by a painter who had the misfortune of getting misled onto a detour. The return is welcomed by this critic also, but for a somewhat different reason having nothing to do with objections to the vaguely regionalist work. Actually, there is a good chance that when all the sifting and shaking down has been done, Charles Burchfield's place in American art may rest most firmly on the pictures in which he recorded the American scene with a special perception of its character.

Much American (as opposed to New York-International American) painting of the thirties can be remembered only with embarrassment for its obviousness and jingoism. The beauty of Burchfield's Americanism of that period (like Edward Hopper's, in a different way) is that Burchfield as a Midwesterner (like Hopper as an Easterner) assumed no stance but painted honestly and expressively in a way that was possible only to a painter of his temperament and his variety of American experience. The resultant paintings were, and remain, fifty times as American as any doctrinaire work by Wood, Benton or Curry, the doggedly American regionalist trinity.

Burchfield never propagandized for the idea that the soil imparts its virtues to cultivators, and his occasional mild satires, another aspect of regionalism, are his least successful pictures. What Burchfield showed us, while other painters were busy retouching the surfaces of the American scene, was the indomitable life of nature beneath the scrubby overlay created by a generation of Americans who had forgotten how to live with nature but had not yet learned how to live away from it.

Whether or not Burchfield was conscious of this American dilemma in the semi-urbanized United States I do not know, but he certainly expressed it. He was thus a regionalist in a much deeper way than those men who hunted out the picturesque superficies of a locale and grafted onto them a set of preconceived notions as to what its character should be—a character that had died with Tom Sawyer's adolescence. In America's trying awkward age—from the depression to Pearl Harbor—Burchfield knew what kind of place he was painting.

The thesis behind these paintings—a thesis that Burchfield did not formulate, but which he understood better than did the painters who tried to formulate it and failed—is not valid today. It had to do with a kind of American provincialism that disappeared with the war, to be replaced perhaps by another kind of provincialism, but which disappeared nevertheless. The Burchfields of latest date in the Whitney retrospective five years ago were efforts to synthesize the fantasy of earlier works with the poetic realism of the vanished thirties and early forties, and they just didn't come off. One of our best painters seemed to be left standing nowhere.

For that reason it is good to find Burchfield the nature fantasist back in his timeless world. He is less specifically an American painter than he was, unless we insist upon believing that Americans have a special sensitivity to the swamps, woods, hills and skies of the wilderness. But he is expressing fully and powerfully the mystical love of nature that infused more delicately his earliest fantasies and more subtly his American scene. As a fantasist he has come back home, and his joy at returning is good to see.

January 8, 1961

THE ORGANIZATION OF FIREWORKS:
Conrad Marca-Relli.

The American paintings and sculptures sent to Moscow in 1959 were a capsule summary of American art since 1928, and hence covered the period of change during which this country shifted from belated impressionism to a limited form of self-examination known as regionalism and finally, after intermediate stages, produced an internationally recognized school of abstraction. An admirably objective committee shied at neither currently deflated nor currently inflated reputations in assembling a group of paintings that may be properly evaluated a hundred years from now. But at the moment, any objective observer could hardly fail to find the abstractions the most attractive spots in the show.

What accounts for this attraction? To what extent is attractiveness *per se* valid as an esthetic quality that will weather? (Grant Wood looked pretty attractive thirty years ago.)

The painting I found myself spending the most time with was Conrad Marca-Relli's "Pamplona," a title that means nothing except possibly to the painter, serving only as an identifying tag for a big, bright, vivacious composition in blacks, whites and modified yellows, the last turning to orange in a spot or two, with some dull reds and inconspicuous dark blues here and there.

Now, abstract painters have their own little civil war, a cul-de-sac engagement in the larger and endless romantic-classic conflict. At one extreme the abstract expressionists believe in effects of spantaneity, freedom, direct attack—the slash, the wide sweep, the nervous calligraphy, the violent color, the generally untrammeled and wholly personal emotionalism around which the romantic world turns. The family tree, leaving out some big branches and all the little twigs, includes Rubens to Delacroix to van Gogh to de Kooning.

In the other camp there is the classical tradition of Poussin to David to Seurat to Mondrian, in which orderly quiet is preferred to slash and sweep, and confined, rigidly controlled line is preferred to nervous calligraphy, purity to violence.

The classical satisfactions are based on intellectual control and are, generally, impersonal and analytical rather than personal and sensational.

"Pamplona" interested me as an expert manipulation of abstract pattern in which some of the merits of both ways of thinking, or feeling, are harmoniously incorporated. I enjoyed what I think of as the precision of its pattern. But this is exactly the point at which descriptive words such as "precision" become relative to the point of meaninglessness, and the critic begins to invent terminologies in the way that is so irritating.

It could be said that the composition of "Pamplona" is a precise and sensitively balanced relationship of interlocking void or blank areas with black or colored areas of varying densities, but that is not much more than could be said of a jigsaw puzzle. It could be said that this is no jigsaw puzzle since the shapes are planned with such nicety of contrast—angular here, curving there, flowing and spreading elsewhere, and intensely compact yet elsewhere—but this would not be saying anything that anybody cannot see for himself if he is ever going to see it at all.

It could be said that the bright scattering of varied yellow shapes is played in counterpoint against the heavier black and red ones. Face to face with the picture such and such a shape could be defended, strictly after the fact, as exactly the shape that in its position plays best against similar or opposing shapes. Finally, the painting offers opportunities for discursive ramifications involving the artist's use of cut cloth pasted onto the canvas to give a different quality to certain edges. Remembering the early use of such technique, we could relish Marca-Relli's adaptation and transformation of ideas introduced in cubist collage and dada play.

All these devices contribute to what I have called the painting's vivacity. As one small terminal branch of various influences ranging back into the history of art as far as you want to go, the painting is a fascinator. But here doubts begin to arise.

All that we have said has to do with the how of art, and not the why. The why of art has to do with humanism, "any system or way of thought or action concerned with the interests and ideals of people." The proposition that "Pamplona" can have much interest except to the specialist or the decorator is a shaky one. Art need not be directed toward the great bleeding heart of humanity, nor can it be directed toward the intellectual standards of the average person (this was the trouble with regionalism), but the painter is lost if his art is so dedicated to theory that it interests a critic, for all the reasons that Marca-Relli interests me, yet becomes meaningless out of context of the history of art.

Rubens or Poussin, David or Delacroix, van Gogh or Seurat are fascinating in historical context, just as Marca-Relli is. But in addition, their art is independent and may speak independently to any human being. The question is whether "Pamplona" can do so, or whether it is only brilliant swordplay for swordplay's sake. The question is whether it is parasitic on, or contributive to, the ideas that are most important humanistically.

I find it hard to believe that in the long historical run "Pamplona" and its kind will be of much more significant interest than descriptions we now have of eighteenth-century firework displays at Versailles. The spectacle is magnificent and in its way indicative of a special aspect of a civilization, its disruption, its excesses, its superficial color. Yet it says nothing of the values that are constant in human endeavor, human hope and human conduct, values that have brought the world back into balance after other periods as desperate as ours.

It is appropriate that, dealing with the values it does, "Pamplona" depends so much for its attraction on size, bravado, impact. It stands out because it insists upon a single dramatic point. Reflective values, which may eventually prove more enduring, seem pallid in the face of its authoritative insistence. It is compellingly attractive. Beyond that, nothing is certain.

November 1, 1959

THEIR SEPARATE WAYS:
Jack Levine and Philip Guston.

Jack Levine and Philip Guston emerged as very young painters of great promise during the depression years of the nineteen thirties, and both, having long since fulfilled their promise, are currently conspicuous artists at two conceptual poles.

For anyone who remembers neither the depression nor the Works Progress Administration, let us identify this government agency. Its program of public works included many new buildings, and it was revolutionary in recognizing, officially, American artists as human beings engaged in a legitimate occupation. It not only commissioned murals for its buildings and for already existing buildings, but also subsidized easel paintings, most of which have become storage problems. Both Levine and Guston were among its protégés.

All this seems a long time ago, although neither of these artists can be described as old men in January, 1960, except by the most impertinent whippersnappers of a generation of painters spawned in an age of mad prosperity. Both are in mid-career, at points of no return and with enough working years ahead to allow them to become major disappointments, or to establish them among the permanently significant names in American painting. Although they have developed in wildly different directions, they are both at precarious stages in their developments—as any stage in the development of a painter is, I suppose, precarious.

Recently in this column I expressed my willingness to plump for Guston as the most rewarding of abstract expressionist painters, a position I continue to hold. But a current exhibition of twenty-nine recent paintings, all from 1958-59 and representing no startling departures from what we already know, has led me to an attempt to track down the sources of a response that has been spontaneous—felt rather than thought out. The attempt involved recourse to a picture file full of reminders and explanations.

In his early twenties Philip Guston, like Jack Levine, was painting pictures of social consciousness. In 1937 he exhibited a tondo, "Bombardment," as part of a show of the American Artists Congress, intended as an anti-Fascist preachment. "Bombardment" was an elaborately expert swirling composition in which Tintoretto and Siqueiros were apparent influences, polished to a tinny brilliance remindful of the then ubiquitous Thomas Benton.

Three years later the young Guston was busy with murals for W. P. A. projects in New York, and had shifted from the agitated forms of "Bombardment" to a static, geometric manner with the frankest debt to Picasso's classical style of the early nineteen twenties. On the walls of a Queensboro housing project, Guston's Americanized Picassani were ornamentally disposed in attitudes based on the standard W. P. A. concept that American life consisted of 'cello playing, heart examinations, basketball, the operation of pneumatic drills, barn dancing, and the contemplation of engineers' and architects' plans and equipment.

But by the mid-forties his personal and introspective art had begun to emerge. In 1945 a picture called "Holiday" showed a small boy, barefoot and in an undershirt, wearing a paper crown and surrounded by symbols theatrically arranged in the manner of magic realism—a drum holding a rose, a merry-go-round horse, doves on a cornice with a shadowy mother figure beyond, plus such identifying urban Americana as bits of a decaying front porch, a street lamp, some telephone wires and distant radio towers.

Sleep, reverie and inward vision developed as the typical Guston theme. Increasingly abstract, his figures appeared with blindfolds, or with their hands before their eyes, with masks, or stretching gauze between their eyes and those of the observer. More and more curious, more and more arbitrarily designed, more and more suggestive of retirement into a world that we were permitted to watch only from the outside, the paintings lost all hint of social consciousness unless a vestige remained in the repeated symbol of a boy in a paper crown, solemn and puzzled in a world that might be poor and sordid.

I believe that the poetry we—or at least, I—find in Mr. Guston's current totally abstract work depends upon these associations, and on the whole that is an unhappy conclusion of a kind that I had hoped not to reach.

A great painter's progress from period to period invariably shows a weeding out of extraneous youthful devices, along with whatever additions are dictated by personal growth. The latest Titians, the latest Cézannes, in general the latest works of any great painter, are distillations of what has gone before, fulfilled and enriched.

Guston's progress has been steadily into a more and more inner world, but I wonder whether he has not reached a core of such secrecy that what he now paints is meaningless except as the latest stage in the retrospective exhibition that is in our minds when we respond to his work today. I find it hard to believe that from what must be a cul-de-sac he will not turn toward a more generally communicative way of painting, so that a single picture may again stand alone— as may a late Titian, Cézanne, or Renoir—rather than depending on what has gone before. His early figurative "If This Be Not I" can still do that. At 47, can he really look forward without unease to a quarter of a century of the manipulation of the private vocabulary that, arranged and rearranged, carries the secret message twenty-nine times in his current show? His problem is the problem of abstract expressionism in general—where next, if this is the ultimate?

Jack Levine may have his problems, but they are not of this kind, for the world continues to supply him with subjects from its bottomless pit of stupidity, viciousness and corruption. From his early "Feast of Pure Reason," done for the W. P. A. and now in the Museum of Modern Art, he has revealed the shoddiness of our vanities, stripped our intellectuals of their pretensions, deflated our politicians and generally found our civilization wanting.

At 44 his problem is not likely to be Guston's, who has shown that ontogeny may not only repeat but may outstrip phylogeny, but the more usual one of failing to grow within the limitations of the area he has selected for his own. Painters who so fail, frequently try to fill with increased manual dexterity the void left by the shrinkage of an idea. In a picture or two Mr. Levine seems more interested in his brush (a wonderfully facile and obedient brush) than in his subject, but so far this occurs only in his light-hearted satires on classical themes where such showmanship is most appropriate.

Considering that they represent extreme poles of American painting, I doubt very much that Mr. Guston and Mr. Levine can abide one another's work. I would be happier about their prospects over the next twenty years, however, if I thought that on occasion they might draw a little sustenance from one another—Mr. Guston, some of Mr. Levine's respect for the visible world as the artist's province, and Mr. Levine, some of Mr. Guston's feeling for the mystery that lies beneath what we see.

January 3, 1960

RENUNCIATION AS ESTHETICS:
Mark Rothko.

Mark Rothko is a Russian-born American painter who for the last ten years has devoted his energy to painting hazy-edged rectangles of color that float in space of another color.

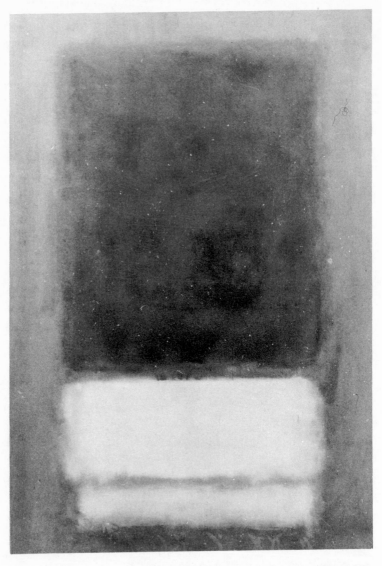

MARK ROTHKO: *OLD GOLD OVER WHITE*, 1956. 68″ x 46″.
Oil on canvas. Collection of Mr. & Mrs. Roy R. Neuberger,
New York.

Any black and white illustration of a Rothko is pointless, since it can yield only a gray shape or two. But color aside, an even greater limitation in getting an idea of what a Rothko looks like except in the presence of the painting itself, is the question of size. Eight feet is a modest dimension in Rothko's current work, and fifteen is no surprise. Any physical dimension, it appears, more and more tethers this artist whose concept is based on the infinite expansion of minimum forms.

The phenomenon of giantism in contemporary painting may sometimes be only a bid for attention (as it also was in the outsize academic canvases of the nineteenth century Salons). But Rothko is one of those painters to whose art large size is intrinsic, as much as color or any other element —and so increasingly that size begins to take on the character of abnormality, an uncontrollable process that has already gone beyond reasonable limits yet gives no sign of stopping of its own accord.

The most curious thing is that there is an inverse ratio between the progressive simplicity of Rothko's style, as far as its forms and colors are concerned, and the size of his paintings. During the past two years he has increasingly rejected the glowing halated colors of the work we have thought of as his most typical, and has reduced the contrasts in his paintings toward the point of lowest visibility. And yet, while he has been pruning away at his palette, painting in sooty and red-brownish neutral tints, reducing his value contrasts (always in the direction of darks) to such an extent that he must call on textural differences to help differentiate between one rectangle and another—while this process of reduction has gone on, the paintings have grown bigger and bigger, so that there is less and less to see on

more and more area. The logical end of the process would
be the painting of uniform colorless tone and infinite size,
before which one would sit looking at nothing and looking at
it beyond the horizon in whatever direction.

Such a conclusion is only partially an absurdity, for the
absurdity is already being approached step by step toward
the point where physical factors must put a stop to things.
And there is nothing to put a stop to the other half of the
idea, the concept that the less an artist says, the more he
says. Whatever other interest Rothko's painting does or does
not hold, there is always the side-interest of watching his
relationship to those critics who are convinced that he is a
truly great artist and who, at this rate, might eventually have
either to confess that the less-is-more theory is subject to
the law of diminishing returns, or to defend a finally inde-
fensible canvas.

The more important thing will be to watch Rothko, who
has never been content to stand still, who is a thoughtful
artist and an imaginative one, as he continues to explore
within the rigorously simplified area he has set for himself.
What will he do next?—since he seems to have brought himself (almost literally) to a blank wall in his largest and
latest and simplest paintings.

Offering an explanation for Rothko's progressive rejection
of all the elements that are the conventional ones in painting, such as line, color, movement and defined spatial relationships, one of his most fervent admirers among critics
states that "(Rothko's) paintings disturb and satisfy partly
by the magnitude of his renunciation."

This is nothing but highflown nonsense if we begin with
the assumption that the audience for painting today is any-

thing but an extremely specialized one. But it does make sense if we understand to what degree the painter today has become a man whose job it is to supply material in progressive stages for the critic's esthetic gymnastics, a distressing cart-before-the-horse relationship that has a kind of bastard legitimacy in a day when other arts supply most of the needs that painting used to supply and leave painting only its more esoteric functions. In such a situation it is quite natural that the critic may be tempted to find most in the painter who says least, since that painter leaves most room for esthetic legerdemain.

We are also told that Rothko's art is essentially humanistic because his paintings "serve as echoes of our experience" by the simple process of supplying a decorative silence. It is true that in a room where Rothko's largest and most monochromatic murals hang on every side, the air of solemnity is impressive enough. The weightiness of the color and the hugeness of the surrounding rectangles suggest the ritual symbols of a harsh and primitive religion. But after all, this is only the creation of a general ambience in which it is easier than usual to release and examine for ourselves whatever we are able to bring.

This may mean successful decoration but I do not see how it can mean great painting. The great painters are those who enlarge, clarify or intensify our experience through some kind of exchange. When a painter does this to a particularized extent, as Rothko may be said to do by supplying an ambience, there is not much point in forcing things to pretend that he does so to a cosmic one. It is a considerable tribute to any painter to say, as one can say of Rothko, that his art stimulates a kind of self-receptiveness in the observer. In saying so much more, his cultists vitiate his considerable powers by calling attention to his limitations.

January 22, 1961

VIOLENCE, MYSTERY, EVOCATION:
Three Contemporary Artists and Their Coming to Terms with the World.

The dilemma facing young artists of creative force today is whether to enter the field of total abstraction with the certainty of being in vogue at the moment and the probability of finding themselves in an impasse in the immediate future, or to explore new paths toward uncertain goals. Three painters who may be taken as superior representatives of some general exploratory directions are Antonio Saura, a Spaniard who lives in Cuenca; Octave Landuyt, a Fleming who lives in Ghent; and Leon Golub, an American who lives in Paris. They are dedicated, respectively, to violence, to mystery, and to what I take to be an evocation of the past as seen through the troubles of the present.

All are good painters, but different. Let us take a look:

The impression when you walk into an exhibition of paintings by Antonio Saura is that you are being assaulted. And by the time you leave, you may feel pretty badly battered, for Saura seems not so much to paint as to attack his canvas in a murderous paroxysm that carries each blow to the observer at full force.

It is easy to imagine the painter howling as he uses his brush like a broadaxe to gash out huge black wounds, and these spurt black blood: paint spatters from them in streams and gobbets, circumstantial evidence of fury in the creation of images of brutality and corruption.

Without the addition of a few final gashes these images might seem totally abstract, for they are slung together in areas that would not be easily identifiable as torsos or heads. But with a smaller weapon Saura carves into the palpitant mass an enormous butchered eye, a flattened nose with nostrils split and opened up, a mouth spread wide as if by an instrument of torture to reveal broken teeth that grind in anguish.

Amateur psychiatrists might conclude that such paintings were created in the double and doubly perverse ecstasy of the sadist and the masochist combined, on the theory that as an artisan the painter inflicts the anguish yet as an artist he suffers it through the image with which he is identified. And certainly any admirer of the religious art of the Renaissance with its serene and noble Christs will be appalled to find a monstrously deformed and hideously butchered figure entitled "Crucifixion" and a similar one with a crown of thorns labeled "Ecce Homo."

But Saura has explained that he thinks of the figure of Christ in such paintings not as a symbol or representation of Christ but as an individual. Certainly he gives little evidence of concern with problems of good and evil. He has an almost fanatic obsession with the spectacle of pain, which is only partially countered by his *frissons* of revulsion against the degradation of cruelty.

The ugliness of Saura's images (always remembering that "ugly" and "beautiful" are relative terms that may even apply

Antonio Saura: *ECCE HOMO,* 1960. 93″ x 75″. Oil on canvas. Courtesy Pierre Matisse Gallery, New York.

simultaneously to the same image in art) can be defended, if defense is necessary, by the precedent of the twisted and putrescent body of Grünewald's Christ in the Isenheim Crucifixion. And that tired old word "compassion" is bound to be hauled out for application here. It does not apply. Nor should Saura be compared, as he inevitably is, to his countryman of a century and a half ago who recorded the brutalities of the Napoleonic invasions in Spain with such despairing objectivity.

One of Goya's records of factual horror is called "This I Saw." Saura's invented apotheoses of horror might be called "These I Relish," and it is in fact this relish that gives the pictures their extraordinary force. But the amateur's sadist-masochist conclusion would be as false as a sociological-compassionate one, and "relish" is too small a word to describe the artist's excitement in communicating an intense emotionalism through forms that are blood brothers to the noncommunicative ones of abstract expressionism.

Esthetically Saura's paintings have the rush and the immediate impact that are paramount virtues of action painting, but spiritually they also catch the observer up with brutal directness and give him a thorough, if non-specific, emotional shaking. Saura throws us into the snake pit. By contrast, even the most highly charged of his abstract expressionist relatives offer us a tour past the glass panes of the snake house in the zoo.

Octave Landuyt, the Fleming, is technically Saura's opposite. His canvases also are large, but they are painstakingly executed in brilliant colors built up through multiple glazes of transparent pigment until they glow like stained glass. He may present us with monstrous heads the size, and very much the shape, of casks, or with invented insects many feet high supporting odd faceted growths. But his latest paintings are what he calls "Essential Surfaces" with such subtitles as "organ coral," "eye," "wings," "coral rock," "vegetal sun" or "vegetable form."

OCTAVE LANDUYT: *PRESENCE IMMOBILE*, 1959. 54″ x 38″. Oil on board. Collection of Mr. & Mrs. Harold Dubilier, New York.

More than anything else to which they can be compared, these resemble blow-ups of medical details in super-color photography, sometimes of diseased livers, sometimes of anatomical cross-sections, always of surfaces in which illusionistic bumps, swellings, pittings and cordings look so real that one must touch them to be certain whether the surface is flat or whether a bit of actual relief has been strengthened by painted shadows and highlights. Landuyt is a master of illusionist technique and is most closely related to surrealism among recent movements. But more than that he is an independent fantasist whose closest relative is his countryman Bosch of nearly five centuries ago.

Now Mr. Golub:

A prominent member of the Chicago group who acquired the tag of monster-painters, he produces oversize male figures in a technique that makes them resemble the remains of images once complete but now only partially legible on chipped, peeling, eroded and scoured frescoed walls. Using a combination of oil and lacquer, he capitalizes on inherent suggestions of flow and clotting so that a painting may end with the general silhouette of a figure in filmy transparent color, upon which gobbets of raised pigment have been applied, like multi-layered islands of paint that have resisted the decay of years on denuded, stained wall surfaces.

Mr. Golub is not easy to relate to a tradition or a school, as Señor Saura is to expressionism or M. Landuyt to fantastical invention, but by straining a point we could connect him with the ideals of monumental calm associated with Masaccio in the early Italian Renaissance.

But in contrast with these ideals, Golub gives us figures that appear to have been brutalized by more than a deteriorated surface. The massive bodies may be limbless, bloated

Leon Golub: *HORSEMAN*, 1958. 84″ x 36″. Oil and lacquer on canvas. Collection of Mrs. Herbert S. Greenwald, Chicago.

or deformed as if by forces which, although they have been overcome, have left the victims inert and dulled, slow and heavy of movement and of thought.

Visually the differences between these painters will strike anybody. They share no common denominators of color, texture or pattern, and they may at first seem to contrast equally in spirit. Yet they do share a common spiritual denominator: all of them accept violence, corruption, decay or pathologies as facts that must be recognized as foundational in life, facts that become tolerable only if man can serve himself with them as a purge, circumstances that must be experienced before we can "lose ourselves in a mystical void" as Señor Saura has written or in the spectacle of fantasy that M. Landuyt offers us, or in Mr. Golub's evocation of the calm of the past without denial of a ruptured and sinister present.

Like it or not, this is the world of the majority of neofigurative painters who have been unable to accept the intellectual precision or the random emotionalism of abstraction. It is no wonder that they appeal less than the practitioners of a more cheerful or more elegant art.

March 7 and March 12, 1961

ART, DUTY AND PLEASURE:
The Case of James Kearns.

Let us consider for a moment the case of James Kearns, an artist who says that he wants to deal with "the total human being," with "the imponderables of life itself," and who has thus chosen a hard row to hoe as well as one that is avoided by most painters and most of the art public today. Mr. Kearns' art is not easy to like, and part of the question concerning him is whether we are under any obligation to try to like it. He holds staunchly to a position from which he must force his way against the current of fashion if he is to get anywhere. He is committed to subject matter that actively bores some people, offends others and interests only a few. He offers no novelties to the public that takes novelty like dope, nor does he offer anything much that is new (newness and novelty not being synonymous). What he tries to say in terms of our time about the condition of a beleaguered yet heroic humanity makes him disastrously vulnerable to comparison with giants who have said it magnificently in terms of theirs—Rembrandt, Goya and Daumier, specifically.

"I want to talk about people in my work," he says, and to do so he has designed an unpleasantly stumpy, dwarf-legged and broad-bodied race of men, globular-headed with lined faces and sunken eyes. His "total human being" has nothing to do with the ideal human being of the Greeks on one hand or with wild, disordered, romantic beauty on the other.

Elegance and decorative attraction are essentially antithetical to the spirit of his work, and so would be any emphasis on technical flair. Certainly, at this stage of Kearns' development he is in no danger on these scores. He appears still to be wrestling, from picture to picture, with his means of expression. He seldom gets his opponent's shoulders all the way down to the mat, and then not for long; he tends to crowd his large pictures not only with lumpy figures but with an excess of lumpy symbolism, although in some fine, strong drawings, he shows what kind of artist he may be.

Naïvely or cynically, we may ask why he does not shift

JAMES KEARNS: *EQUESTRIAN*, 1957. 24″ x 36″. Charcoal. Courtesy Grippi Gallery, New York.

to another kind of painting, one for which an audience has already been conditioned. The audience today for what Mr. Kearns is trying to do has nearly dwindled away, a fact that he recognizes when he says that he "can't reject society" although "no matter how hard I try to find my place, society may reject me."

To the totally unrecognized artist, Kearns may seem to be doing fairly well. He came to the attention of Ben Shahn, no mean sponsor, when Shahn and Joe Jones, as a two-man jury, awarded him first prize in a local show in Morristown, N. J., in 1955. The prize was $100 worth of merchandise from a clothing shop beneath the gallery. Then last year, Shahn chose Mr. Kearns as his most promising "new talent" when

Look magazine asked four eminent modern painters to make selections. (Stuart Davis selected Joseph Glasco, Andrew Wyeth selected Robert Bliss, and Hans Hofmann, bringing up the avant-garde, selected Alfred Leslie.) This year Kearns made his first sale to a museum when the Whitney purchased his "Cat's Cradle" with $900 from the Neysa McMein Fund. Three years ago, the Museum of Modern Art accepted as a gift (not from the artist) a large Kearns drawing, "The Ring," but has exhibited it only once, perfunctorily and courteously as a new acquisition.

For the rest, Kearns has a handful of ardent admirers who purchase frequently. Thus he is making a grade of sorts. But the big market is not yet within his sights, and the question we are examining is why this should be so, when this market has patronized so many artists of less substantial merit.

What it comes down to is that Kearns does not offer us a pleasurable art. He has neither the ornamental flair, the voguish decorator quality of the painters who paint easy-come easy-go, nor the old-fashioned associational appeal that continues to make much figurative painting a steady seller on a quiet market.

Falling within neither of these classifications, neither does Kearns fall somewhere in between. He falls outside—in an area where very few painters, Ben Shahn being a conspicuous exception, have been able to make a go of it. It is an area where social consciousness is a large element in the investigation of human nature and where human nature is more important than esthetic theory, where inner content is more important than attractive surface, and where unless you are very good indeed you are not nearly good enough.

Is Kearns good enough? Not yet, with Rembrandt, Goya

and Daumier as yardsticks. Will he get there? Possibly, if he can manage to survive as a painter while surviving as a physical entity who must find means to feed and shelter himself and his family. To get down to brass tacks, do I enjoy his work? To tell the truth, not very much.

But "enjoy" is a loose word. Going from Kearns' rather depressing exhibition in a small and unfashionable gallery to the show of Adolph Gottlieb at a large and expensive one, I "enjoyed" from the point of view of visual excitement, of curiosity stimulated and temporarily satisfied, watching Mr. Gottlieb perform with his usual brilliance this year's variations of his usual rope trick. At a similar gallery I "enjoyed" José Guerrero's performance, in which a great deal of bright color was thrown around with a typical combination of facility and abandon. Recognizing the name of one purchaser, I made a telephone call that verified the supposition that the big bang was destined to ornament a wall of a certain suburban orangerie combined with a living room and a swimming pool, where it will look beautiful and a Kearns would not. But that is exactly the point: Kearns is not interested first in how his pictures "look."

Should he be? And since his pictures are so often ugly, should we reject them or should we make hopeful concessions? What is the nature and degree of our obligation to patronize, on faith, a painter whose intention is nobler than his achievement in contrast with painters who paint more attractively from a lesser premise?

Kearns' art is evidence that in the arts today the stuff of life is likely to be the kiss of death, and that any artist who deals with it is a brave man or a fool. But we owe a fighting chance to this kind of nonconformist—the chance, simply, to work for an audience, for it is only through an audience that he can show whether or not he is up to the big job he has set himself.

December 5, 1960

ON INNOCENCE:
With Reference to Philip Evergood.

Philip Evergood is a painter whom I have for a long time done my level best to understand and enjoy. But I am ready to say that either I don't understand him, which could leave him a much better artist than he appears to me, or that I do understand him and he is not as good as his admirers, who fortunately outnumber me, think he is. I hope I am wrong, since Evergood is a painter whose every stated premise should make him the kind of artist we need and need badly, one who draws his material directly from the life we see around us and is eager to share his ideas, and thus enlarge ours, by painting in terms that people can understand.

The problem lies in the nature of innocence. Innocence is a most perishable quality, and the surest sign that an individual has lost it is his awareness of innocence as something discernible in others or in his past self. Innocence may be lost unhappily through corruption or, happily enough, through the natural course of events called experience. But once it is gone it is gone for good, and any effort to return to it, or to cling to it, or to feign it in the interest of self-deception or of deceiving others, is disastrous.

The art of true innocents, those we call the "modern prim-

PHILIP EVERGOOD: *SELF PORTRAIT WITH DIVINING ROD*, 1960. 20″ x 14″. Oil on canvas. Owner: Mr. & Mrs. Alvin P. Gutman. Photograph courtesy ACA Gallery, New York.

itives" or the folk artists of any time, is an art that we enjoy
from a contradictory point of view, as sophisticates. It is this
distance that gives innocent art its character for us, and the
greater our degree of sophistication, the greater the appeal
of the works of innocent art is likely to be. Their every technical or spiritual approach to our studio standards of excellence weakens them.

What Evergood seems not to realize is that this knife cuts
both ways. Not an innocent (his background includes Eton,
Cambridge, Paris, London, extensive travel, and a wide
variety of American adventures), he chooses to work in a
style that borrows heavily from the art of innocents. His
every departure from the studio standards of which he is
capable (and has from time to time applied) weakens the
force of paintings that try for forcefulness through devices
that are forceful in the painting of genuine primitives. Even
his signature, which he writes conspicuously oversize as
primitive painters are likely to do on their work, and in an
odd scrawl, is a detraction.

Let no one try to use in rebuttal the fact that the cubists
and the fauves found in African sculpture an inspiration for
twentieth-century art. After the briefest forays into fairly
direct imitations of African forms, they departed into highly
theoretical and civilized directions having nothing to do with
African fetishism. Nor did Paul Klee, fascinated by every
kind of primitive art, including the art of children, use its
forms except as keys to the door of a world so hyper-civilized
that it has been called one of "fourth-dimensional innocence."

I cannot feel that Evergood has done anything of the kind.
The pseudo-primitive elements of his highly individual style
simply have never fused with his messages of social significance, and faced by his paintings I always feel that I must

grope to discover hints of the intelligent modern man who created them. He is like a college professor I know who adopts an unnatural folksiness, who says "ain't got none" and leaves his hair uncombed to assure us that he is a real guy, not the esthete who hides behind this facade.

The objection would not be worth making if Evergood had not shown, in parts of many paintings and in the whole of one or two, what a superb painter and poet he can be. It is almost redundant at this stage to mention one more time his portrait of his mother, a painting that may remain an isolated masterpiece in the art of the mid-twentieth century.

But in contrast with the tender and genuine sentiment of this painting, the typical Evergood is infected with a kind of inflated folksiness, a we-are-all-just-common-fellows-here-together attitude. Why does Evergood feel impelled to do this? Why all the disfiguring attitudinal veneer? By all the evidence, beneath this veneer he is an artist concerned with life, with speaking to people, with sharing his convictions and perceptions, which are strong and meaningful. Why does he choose to speak in so self-consciously ungrammatical a way, in sentences of such distorted syntax? This is beyond me, and it distresses me. He is like a man who hides behind an exaggerated gawkiness. This I will never understand.

The adoption of what I take to be a consciously gauche style stands between what the artist intends to say and what the observer understands him to say. Take as an example the picture "My Forebears Were Pioneers," painted in 1940, one of Evergood's most frequently exhibited and illustrated paintings.

Evergood explains that after the hurricane of 1938 he saw "this beautiful, austere old lady" who, being of pioneer stock, met the "complete destruction of her house and trees" in the imperturbable spirit of her grandfathers who had fought Indians.

Yet my own response to this picture has always been that it shows a rather vacant and smug looking old woman and that the desolation against which she is placed is more suggestive of the deterioration of a society over several generations than of the continuance of its strength. The title "My Forebears Were Pioneers" would thus be an ironical one. By this interpretation I had always thought of the picture as one of Mr. Evergood's successes. By his own, it would be for me a failure. Granting my own fallibility, I have found that my response to the picture has been the general one among people who know it but do not know the painter's stated intention.

But there are always for certain critics certain painters who don't come through, and these painters can include—for me— such recognized giants as William Blake, who occasionally seems a cousin to Evergood. This puts Mr. Evergood in the best of company, and we may assume that the loss is mine.

May 1 and July 17, 1960

DEATH WITHOUT GODS:
A Note on Leonard Baskin.

Leonard Baskin's art, merely described, must sound gloomy, morbid or, at best, romantically melancholy. It is none of these, although his recurrent theme is death. One wonder-

LEONARD BASKIN: *GLUTTED DEATH*, 1959. 40″ x 26″. Ink
drawing. Collection of Mr. M. J. Stewart. Photograph courtesy
Grace Borgenicht Gallery, New York.

ful and terrible figure, which exists in drawings and in
bronze, called "Glutted Death," is a figure part skeleton, part
shrunken flesh, with a mask half recognizable and half obliterated by scarring or decay; it thrusts toward us the horror
of its packed and swollen belly.

An ink drawing of a dead crow is at first glance an inchoate mass of broad conflicting brush strokes, until the
sharp dead beak emerges, and then the poor rigid legs and
warped claws. Unlike other familiar studies of dead birds—
Dürer's, for instance—with their description of feathers and
anatomy, this one is of a creature once sleek and powerful
but now broken and decayed, its scheme of plumage and
tendons disrupted and meaningless.

Yet if death is Baskin's most frequent theme, it is insepar-
able from the theme of man's dignity in the face of his own
mortality. Without offering hope of the spirit's winged escape
from carcass to paradise, Baskin implies its triumph over
death through recognition of death's omnipotence, accept-
ance of the body's corruption, and insistence upon life's
nobility. His human figures are never beautiful in the classical sense of perfected proportions or the romantic one of
loveliness doomed to destruction. His human beings are
short legged, thick torsoed, bald; nothing in their nakedness
suggests the pleasures of the flesh or what is thought of as
the beauty of life. But they stand with a firmness that is in
itself a kind of immortality.

Again and again in Baskin's work the suggestion of Egyptian sculpture is strong, without any parasitism on Egyptian
forms. The relationship is a natural one between an ancient
concept that identified the materiality of a carved image with
assurance of the soul's eternal life, and a modern concept
by which the act of creation is a record of man's determina-

tion to hold his position at the center of a universe in which he is no longer sure of his gods.

It is important to reiterate that Baskin's final comment has little to do with the terribleness of life or even the terribleness of death, and nothing to do with resigned pessimism or blind optimism. He is concerned with neither happiness nor sorrow. He is concerned with the legitimacy of life and the importance of man's obligation to accept its continuity as meaningful in spite of its brevity for the individual.

March 20, 1960

COWS AND SCHMOOS:
The Romantic Sensibility of Jean Dubuffet.

Jean Dubuffet is a wildly contradictory painter. By every postulate of what we used to call beauty his work is coarse and ugly. By similar intellectual and moral postulates it is infantile, degenerate, brutal, capricious, psychotic, or at best blatantly nonsensical.

On the basis of individual works, Dubuffet might be any one of these things. On the basis of his total production he is none of them. Perhaps we should expect a first-rate painter to be able to sum up what he has to say in a single picture. But for some reason painters are seldom able to do so today, and Dubuffet, especially, demands an over-all acquaintance with his work before a single picture makes full sense.

One of his saving characteristics is that laughter swells and billows through his art. The laughter is sometimes ribald but it is never desperate. Dubuffet says again and again that the world is in a mess, but that living in it is still a mysterious experience. He states with Gallic wit this good Gallic attitude that has helped France to revitalize herself more than once.

On this idea, an argument could be developed to make Dubuffet the most important French painter since the disasters of the early forties. He is frequently given this title, but not for the reasons that make him seem important to me. He impresses me as an artist of romantic sensibilities and one of paradoxically tender humanism beneath his apparent rejection of humanistic sentiment; this would make him an artist who stands at the head of the movement that rejects the intellectualism of contemporary painting yet does so by offering a positive art instead of the art of negation that typifies the bulk of painting classifiable as romantic today.

Establishing, no doubt, a world's record for the standing mental broad jump, I find myself thinking of Rembrandt while looking at Dubuffet in certain characteristic pictures. Perhaps this idea had better be approached gradually:

Dubuffet was born in 1901, studied painting as a youth, gave it up as a young man and went into business—wine. About 1942 he began to paint again and in 1944 he held his first exhibition, at the age of 43. His pictures at that time were bright expressionist inventions, drawn in a pseudo- or neo-primitive style. Most critics take these more seriously than I can. They seem to me to be happy, high-grade clowning, although that is nothing against them. Happy, high-grade clowning as such is all right with me.

But Dubuffet changed just after the war. He continued

to translate into his own manner elements from the drawings of savages, children, and insane people, as well as the
universal symbols used in back-fence scrawlings. But his
gaiety and vivacity were replaced by a sinister brutality.
His horrendous textures and grimy colors—the textures and
colors of clotted mud, ash and cinders, the cold aftermath
of destruction—seemed either a last-ditch effort to salvage
a little something from the end of a civilization, or a bitter
rejection of the society that had brought things to such a
pass.

"Terrifying," now the weariest adjective in the critical
vocabulary, had just been discovered as a catch-all, and we
called Dubuffet "terrifyingly witty," "wittily terrifying," "terrifyingly innocent" and "terrifyingly sophisticated." It was
safe to say almost anything about him, because nobody was
certain just what was happening except that in pictures asso-
ciable with death and destruction Dubuffet seemed alive and
creative.

Since then he has abandoned his dried-mudpie textures
and has grown steadily more inventive, somewhat more conventional and infinitely more elaborate technically. He still
uses paste-ons from time to time, and may even go so far
as to concoct an image entirely from dried leaves, a nominal
continuation of dada and surrealism. But for the most part
he is increasingly a pure painter. His colors have become
richer; into a general tonality of grays and browns he introduces the subtlest lavenders, reds, greens and golds. He
may give over one of his exquisitely colored canvases to a
caricature of a cow, an animal that fascinates him with its
grotesque form and its stupid complacency, or he may present us with a gigantic, bulbous head remindful of a diseased
potato, an unidentifiable creature from the depths of the

sea, and a monstrous human mutation, all at the same time. Still leavened with humor, this concoction will never be for some people anything more than an oversize schmoo.

And a schmoo it is, in part. The schmoo, that spectral and jovial little comic, must have satisfied some need for us. Otherwise he would never have achieved such wide popularity. His offbeat, urbane personality, at once funny and vaguely menacing, made him a folk character in the twentieth-century legend.

A combination of humor and menace is present also in Dubuffet's art. Recently he has denied the humor, probably because it was overemphasized in early efforts to figure him out. Currently we exaggerate the element of menace, in line with the "new images of man" idea that art today must necessarily reflect the most ominous aspects of our time. Fetishism, magic and sorcery are also parts of the Dubuffet compound. But beyond these there is a strong element of pathos. I am trying to avoid another tired word, compassion, but here it is, for Dubuffet's art is compassionate and gentle in spite of the first impression of grossness and violence that it makes on an unaccustomed eye.

The connection with Rembrandt is explainable on a double score, tenuous as it is. (A current may be conducted through very thin wires.) Rembrandt's brown canvases yield their coloristic richness only gradually, as do Dubuffet's. Furthermore, Rembrandt's textures, with rough, heavily loaded lights against thinly painted passages, may have a more than coincidental connection with Dubuffet's. His—Rembrandt's—compassion for the human condition, which led him to choose the aged, the poor and the infirm as his models instead of the young, the happy and the conventionally beautiful, has some kind of parallel in Dubuffet's inven-

JEAN DUBUFFET: *LE SENTENCIEUX*, 1958. 38¾″ x 36″. Oil on canvas. Collection of Mr. & Mrs. Elias Pinto, New York: Photograph courtesy Pierre Matisse Gallery, New York.

tion of bloated and deformed figures delineated on surfaces suggesting erosion and decay.

Without pushing this any further—and God forbid that on the basis of these comments anybody should ever call Dubuffet "The Modern Rembrandt"—we can admit the possibility that the response of a twentieth-century Frenchman may overlap that of a seventeenth-century Dutchman when he looks at his fellow man, and that resemblances of color and technique that seem forced in comparison may be accounted for because they serve comparable ends of expression.

November 11 and November 15, 1959

A Satire:

DELICIOUS INNOVATOR:

Scoop Interview with a Shy Revolutionary.

We took a long-awaited opportunity last week to interview an artist who has been making a quiet sensation in art circles lately—Miss Amy Crush, whose paintings executed entirely in raspberry jam have contributed significantly to contemporary explorations of new methods and materials. We would like to share this experience with our readers.

Miss Crush received us in the charming studio apartment she has created at the bottom of an abandoned elevator shaft ("I have always liked high ceilings," she explains) to show us some of her work and describe some of her objectives. A slight, soft-spoken person who has been painting in secret for twenty years, Miss Crush was modest about her achievement.

"Anybody could have done what I have done—I suppose," she said. "In the early days before I could afford to buy all the materials I needed, it was mostly a matter of getting out at night and collecting bits of jam from old pots before the trash men arrived—and," she added, with a little chuckle of recollection, "of controlling one's appetite at the same time."

Miss Crush describes herself as a "slow worker." For one thing, she points out, she is forced to limit her creative activities to the winter months because of the fly problem. The summer is given over to contemplation.

Asked how she happened to choose her unusual medium she explained, "Well, like so many other avant-garde painters, I had a thorough academic training, and I wouldn't give anything for it. This was in grammar school, where we did tulip stencils in spring, Santa Clauses at Christmas, and posters for worthy causes, all very illustrative. It seemed terribly restricting at the time, and it did delay full realization of my potential. Frankly, I had never heard of overlapping planes, not to mention spatial interpenetration and simultaneous voids, until I was 13 and overheard other children talking about them in the schoolyard.

"I discovered my personal medium one day after I had begun painting on my own, many years later," she went on. "I was working on a portrait of a friend and I just couldn't get the effect I wanted. I finally got it by touching up the cheeks with a bit of currant jelly—just as an experiment, not thinking it would lead to all this.

"Once I had begun, I found myself depending more and

more on preserved fruit for my effects—orange marmalade in blonde hair, for instance—until finally I realized that I was using more edible pigments, as I like to call them, than ordinary ones, and I thought why not 'go all the way' so I did. And that was that," she added with a little gesture of dismissal.

However, Miss Crush's experiments are not so lightly dismissed by the art world. "Fascinating," "revolutionary," and "adorably luscious" are some of the descriptions used. No less a personage than Nightingale Sweeney has called these jam-paintings "the immediately exteriorated expression of potential inner experience"—in other words, almost good enough to eat. More conservative critics have objected to the "sticky" effect of Miss Crush's medium. Others, paradoxically, have found it "crusty."

"What my critics don't understand," Miss Crush objected, "is that while other painters have early, middle and late periods, I don't—but my paintings do. It's what I call 'inherent development.' A painting has its sticky period, its crusty period, and—well, we'll see. These changes, I like to think, account for some of the natural dynamism that critics have felt in my work without being able to explain it."

The word "crusty" brought a flood of reminiscences. "I used to work on slices of bread," Miss Crush recalled, "and I would still like to do so, but I needed a broader canvas. I tried pancakes and did a few tondos as much as nine inches in diameter, and these were effective, I thought, but like other forward-looking painters I have been much concerned with the concept of the expanding image. That is why I have been using my edible pigments on sponge rubber slabs lately. There's no limit to size and it's as close as I can come to bread, which is still the perfect surface, of course."

Miss Crush showed us some of her earliest paintings, now extremely rare, done entirely in edible pigments ranging through the spectrum. Strawberry, orange, lemon, lime, blueberry, grape and apple butter (for shadows) became her standard palette. "But when I hit on raspberry I knew I really had it," she said, a glow coming into her eye. "And raspberry has more range than you'd suspect," she went on, licking her fingers as she has a habit of doing when discussing her work. "There's red raspberry, black raspberry, fresh raspberry, spoiled raspberry, and of course all the subtle variations between different manufacturers' brands. But what I like most about working with a single flavor is that it gives my work a purity, a kind of ultimate purity I like to believe, that my multi-flavored painting simply did not have."

Miss Crush was reluctant to talk further about herself, but we did get from her the admission that her forthcoming exhibition at the Node Gallery has been passed by the Committee on Exceptional Regulations of the Pure Food Commission. In Miss Crush's field, this is the equivalent of the Nobel Prize. She seems also to have added a term to the French language. "Framboisism" is now up before the French Academy for admission to the next edition of the Nouveau Petit Larousse.

July 2, 1961

PART FOUR:
Collectors and Museums

THE COLLECTOR:

Origin and Examples of the Species.

More people are collecting art today than ever before, and although statistics on their number are unavailable, the yellow pages of the Manhattan Telephone Directory list more than 400 "Art Galleries and Dealers" in ten columns. Since this is almost exactly the same amount of space as that taken by "Bakeries, Retail," we may presume that art runs hot competition to the staff of life in 1961, and that man indeed does not live by bread alone.

The impulses that lead man to eat are well known and easily explained. Those that lead him to collect are equally persistent but more curious and varied. The purpose of this article is to examine them by establishing categories of collectors in an effort to see what the whole thing is about. To do so with any effectiveness, we must first examine the problem in historical depth.

The collector is a breed who appeared in prehistoric times with the first two-legged creature who made himself a little pouch in which he could carry around some pretty but useless pebbles. He survived, even though he would frequently get sidetracked in the middle of a bison hunt when he saw something sparkling on the ground. If it turned out to be a pebble of a kind he didn't have, he felt rewarded although he was left with an empty stomach. Even if the pebble wasn't, after all, unusual, he didn't regret having taken the chance.

At night before going to bed he would get his pebbles out and line them up by the last light of the fire, and contemplate them. They gave him a kind of pleasure not exactly comparable to anything else, although within this pleasure were compounded elements of the unreasonable affection he held for his mate, the wonderment he felt at the rise of the sun every morning, and the excitement he felt when he tried to examine an idea he had recently half-discovered, that he was an entirely different kind of being from the animals and, for that matter, a cut or two above his fellow non-animals whose interests were limited to feeding and breeding.

At first the other members of the tribe thought he was a little crazy. They resented his abandonment of the tribal bison hunts in the pursuit of his hobby, but since he was willing to forego his share of the kill in order to indulge it, they tolerated him. They began thinking this over and became curious, and then impressed. Sometimes before turning in for the night they would ask him if they could see his pebbles. He was always happy to show them, and he discovered in fact that his pleasure in his collection was thus increased.

Some members of the tribe never were able to understand what he saw in pebbles, but others became fascinated and began picking up pebbles for their own pleasure. Soon there was a group of pebble collectors who shared their pleasures with one another.

At this point, collecting was still a philosophical activity. But as the idea spread it began to be affected by many side issues, not all of them good. One of the first questionable ones was the competitive attitude, which in turn led to the commercial virus. The original pebble collector was not happy with a pebble unless he had found it for himself, and he never traded pebbles, as some of the new collectors began to do among themselves.

A further vulgarization of the collecting impulse took place when prestige became involved. Members of the tribe to whom pebbles actually meant nothing could not help noticing that those members to whom pebbles meant a great deal happened also to be the brightest members of the tribe. They began collecting pebbles that looked to them like those in the best collections, and were never able to understand why the experts found them inferior. Defensively they muttered that maybe they didn't know much about pebbles but they knew what kind of pebble they liked.

Before long, some sharp members of the tribe discovered that they could get more bison meat by gathering pebbles and then trading them for portions of the kill than they could by joining the hunt. Thus the dealer was born. He further complicated things by creating a popularity for pebbles of eccentric but philosophically unrewarding shapes, and in the dead of night he would go off and forge pebbles in shapes nature never intended.

With everybody collecting now, and with collections passing from father to son, the pebble pouches began to grow too heavy to carry around. This problem was solved when it fused with a new concept, the concept that great pebbles should be preserved and placed on exhibition as a record for posterity and for the education of the young. The museum was born, and a sickly member of the tribe, the first curator, was appointed to stay home and guard it. He has been doing so ever since, and some of the things he has said and written about pebbles would make your hair stand on end.

The unhappiest offshoot of the curatorial development was the establishment of critical authority. Curators and critics (the first critic was a blind man who convinced the tribe that he had both backward and forward vision) joined forces to impose an esthetic dictatorship, telling people which pebbles were good and which pebbles were bad. This was the final perversion of the philosophical impulse that had led to the whole business.

At just what point the interest in collecting shifted from pebbles to art is anybody's question, but the basic types of collectors have remained essentially unchanged. The informal philosopher who collects art because he needs to have it around to be a whole man, is the direct descendant of the first collector whose pebbles lined up by firelight gave such undefinable pleasure and led to such mysterious extensions of his experience with love, nature, and the human spirit. Lesser types include the gamesman, who collects as a competitive activity; the climber, who collects for prestige; the me too-er, who collects because other people do; the philatelic or stamp-collector type whose goal is to acquire a complete set of typical "examples" in a "balanced collection"; the pack rat, whose standard is quantity; the would-be prince, who covets a work of art for its lineage and by acquiring it establishes himself as an aristocrat; the playboy, who judges art by its capacity to excite the intellectual equivalent of café society; and the speculator, who regards art as a stock to be manipulated on the market.

These types overlap and less than half of them are admirable, yet so great is the power of art to seduce and at the same time to elevate rather than to debauch, that the person who begins to collect for any reason is likely to rise from the least respectable motives toward the only one that means anything—the satisfaction of the spirit. As is well known, collecting is a communicable infection, and the first purchase of a work of art, no matter how casually approached, is usually the symptom of a derangement which will increase in intensity and with which the victim must be prepared to live for the rest of his days. But contradictorily the infection is a nourishing one, and even speculator-collectors have been known to approach a recognition of art for what it is, the tangible expression of the intangible values that men live by.

But since the speculator is the one entirely unworthy and the least frequently redeemed type of art collector, we might write him off first in analyzing the various classifications. Like speculators in any field he operates on the principle of buying cheap and selling high. That his commodity is art is incidental to the fact that it is a commodity. When truly base, he operates with the canny dealer in specious innovations and the kind of critic or curator who, either venal or deluded, inflates a market created in the first place by critics and curators who go about their jobs knowledgeably and honestly. But whether his methods are straightforward or devious, the art speculator is engaged in a kind of investment operation chancy enough to make the betting windows at the race track look like the tellers' windows at the savings bank, or the floor of the Stock Exchange on panic day look like the cool vaults of Fort Knox.

The speculative art market is engaged first in building up contemporary reputations, but it also polishes up for resale faded reputations from the past, and it has no Securities and Exchange Commission to keep a restricting eye upon it. Wildly stimulated at this moment by the upward rush of all art prices, it feeds on excitement and conjecture. But those who know their way around in it are aware that today's novelty is tomorrow's bore, and they buy and sell accordingly.

Since speculation in art is a commercial rather than an esthetic proposition, we may say that those who make money at it deserve this reward for their acumen, and that those who are left holding the bag must accept the fate of the tardy or the gullible. The greatest growth stocks in art, however, have not been purchased on speculation or even as investment. There are collectors who are buying cheap today because they happen to want what they buy and want it for keeps, and who will later find themselves (or more likely their children or grandchildren) in the possession of valuable works of art. But they are not speculators; they are informal-philosopher types who happen to be extraordinarily in phase with their times. They are the people who liked Cézanne enough to buy him fifty or seventy-five years ago when you could have bought everything he painted for what a single fine example might cost now. Who are these people today and what are they buying? Who knows.

The prince-by-purchase collector is at the opposite pole from the speculator. He acquires only gilt-edged stocks, already proven and so valuable that a single share of Rembrandt, coming up for auction this fall, is expected to bring at least a million dollars and could, some collectors believe, bring nearer two million. At prices like this the investment factor ceases to operate independently; a certain amount of passion must be involved. The would-be prince who purchases pictures for their lineage may thus cease to be an aristocrat merely by proxy or by reflection, and become one by marriage as the result of a love match. This is much better.

By comparison, the playboy collector, although he is an interesting figure, is having a go at tiddley-winks both spiritually and financially. The art circles in which he moves, like the comparable social circles of café society, are filled with aristocratic intellectual titles of dubious authenticity or degenerated significance, and the premium is on fashion and novelty. Surface is enough to satisfy such a collector and he builds a flashy collection of the names described as "exciting" in the art columns and, alas, in too many of the exhibitions. Where our princely collector has adopted the Metropolitan Museum as his ancestral castle, the playboy has made the Museum of Modern Art his El Morocco, to the misfortune of that estimable institution.

Both the prince and the playboy are touched with the lust for prestige, although the prince is usually so rich and so stable in prestigious worlds that his collection is only an expected adjunct to his position. But there is also the climber-collector who wants to be sought after by the representatives of the charities and museums to whom his collection is valuable or who, at a higher level, simply wants to move in circles sympathetic to him and whose collection, intelligently formed, can bring to attention the fact that he is worthy of inclusion.

Such collections usually follow models formed in the circle of wealthy, intelligent, well advised and often sensitive people who collect on the philatelic principle. The collections most frequently run from impressionism through Matisse and Picasso, summarizing a development now secure in historical perspective. "I need a Braque" or "I need a blue period Picasso" are typical indications of the philatelic attitude, and when a collection is formed purely on the fill-the-stamp album premise it can be as dull as a stamp album is to the person who regards stamps as something to stick on letters. But when each example is selected because it not only fills a space but offers, as well, something that makes it appeal overpoweringly to the collector, the collection can have a unity and a personality unique to itself in a way that

has put some "philatelic" art collections among the great
private ones of the world just now.

But with supply diminishing and demand increasing, considerable competitive activity is involved in finding the right
picture for the right place. Part of the joy of collecting is
always a frank gloating that the desired object is mine, all
mine—this happens in love, too—but there are collectors for
whom the object is only a trophy. Their collections include
genuinely good pictures because the pictures most competed
for are the ones that have been best proven, but to see them
lined up like tennis cups is distressing to collectors who
would have liked to give them a more appropriate home.
The same holds true of whatever good things find their
way into the hands of a me-too collector. He may be dismissed here as a minor variation of the gamesman. Basically
a dope, the only cups he ever wins he wins by default.

The pack rat is not as bad as he sounds. Oddly enough,
he may be close to our original and informally philosophical
gatherer of pebbles. It is not that he will collect just anything; it is that once he gets interested there is no such
thing as a totally uninteresting work of art for him. No matter how bad it is, it takes its place in context as part of the
vast and continuous expression and record that men have
left of themselves and their times. The pack rat's fascination with everything is not so much a massive unselectivity
as it is a universal recognition. The worst and now least
collected French academicians of the last century become
interesting in context with the best and now most collected
impressionists who revolted against them, even when the
appalling differences between them are most obvious.

There was no such historical-social esthetic to complicate
the original pebble collector's wonderment at something he

found beautiful and inexplicably stirring, any more than there were considerations of speculation and prestige. Very few collectors today can approximate his response in its purity. But the impulse that stirred him and the satisfactions he found are still the foundation upon which the whole complicated business of collecting is based. If it were to vanish, the superstructure it supports would collapse.

August 6, 1961

THE TELEPHONE MYSTERY:

What Do You Do When You Have to Spend a Thousand Dollars for a Painting and Don't Know How?

In a voice that sounded too natural to be part of a hoax, a young woman, or at any rate a woman with a voice that sounded young, called this office around noon one day last week and asked where to go to buy a painting for $1,000 that would supply an appropriate spot of color for an office. Although this initial attack and the subsequent development of the conversation left me a little confused, I retained the impression that the young woman's boss had assigned her this duty as one of those extensions of the secretarial function that include such agreeable chores as watering the office plants and keeping an eye on the tidiness of the place in general.

The idea of a young woman's starting out with $1,000 on such an errand is stimulating to the imagination, but the telephone conversation turned out to be distressing to both parties. I could think of a dozen galleries where $1,000 would buy a good painting as well as a dozen where it would buy only a piece of ruined canvas, and another dozen where it could buy either. I could think of a dozen young painters who for $300 or $400 would sell a painting as good as some of the best that sell at a full thousand, and some others who would sell for $1,000 a painting better than many that sell for as much as $5,000 to $10,000. I could also get out of the contemporary field and think of eighteenth and nineteenth century paintings of minor museum caliber that could be had for $1,000 and there was also the thought of an office hung with a group of first-rate drawings, for $1,000, instead of one painting.

But these thoughts were beside the point, since in his professional capacity it is unethical (and even in his personal one, unwise) for a critic to recommend one gallery or one painter over another to a prospective purchaser, although anyone may deduce what he pleases from a critic's published judgments.

This point the young woman never did understand, although we went over it several times. But if I felt that way, would I supply her with the names of five galleries that handle dependable $1,000 paintings if she promised not to breathe the name of *The New York Times?* This proposal was rejected.

Then how was she to begin, she asked. She had come directly to what she naturally expected to be a source of help after discovering that there are ten columns of listings under Art Galleries and Dealers in the Yellow Pages of the telephone directory.

I suggested that if she were going to drop $1,000 on a

commodity that, she said, she didn't know anything about, and if, in addition, she wasn't even sure what kind of painting she wanted—which she said she wasn't, except that she wanted "something modern"—it might be a good idea to spend a couple of weeks looking around the galleries using current art reviews in this newspaper and elsewhere as some kind of a guide.

But she said no, she not only didn't have a copy of last Sunday's paper but she also didn't have the time. She wanted a painting, she wanted a $1,000 painting, and she wanted it that afternoon. We ended where we began—nowhere.

On the most obvious face of it, it is wonderful that people want to buy paintings in the process of decorating offices, apartments, restaurants and every place else. Yet this incident demonstrates with a purity almost absurd a less encouraging face of this country's new interest in art, a face that has nothing to do with art but everything to do with our passion for conformity and our fear of being left out of the fashionable running. A generation of hard work by colleges and other institutions in devising effective "art appreciation" courses and the skillful adoption of high-pressure publicity techniques by museums has certainly enlarged the knowledgeable audience for painting. But it has also encouraged the production of spurious work by lifting art in this country from the status of something half suspect to the status of something accepted blindly as worthwhile. People now hang paintings on their walls with the idea that somehow something called culture will be exuded for absorption much in the way that they install an efficient humidifier in order to impregnate the air with beneficial moisture for breathing.

This concept of art by which the purchase of a picture becomes instant-education is not entirely new. Pictures on the wall and books on the shelves, whether or not the pictures were seen or the books ever opened, supplied "a cultured atmosphere" for our grandmothers' houses. The trouble today is that mass communications, mass color reproductions, mass museum programs and mass cultural attacks in general when they propagandize for art will be most successful when the product being sold is flashiest. It is much easier to make a bad painting sound good than it is to explain why a good painting *is* good. When this misfortune is compounded by the misconception, peculiar to our century, that only the novel and "original" painting is worthwhile, we finally reach the idea of the standard novelty—the mass product that people think of as something not mass-produced but special, the pseudo-esoteric item for general prestige consumption.

I suspect that that was what my anonymous telephone caller wanted. The chances are that if on her shopping tour she was offered a painting to which she responded naturally she suspected it of being no good, but that if she was offered a splash of paint with a $1,000 price tag she was convinced it was "good" because it resembled all the other splashes of paint she had seen in so many magazines, which she had been told were fare for the elite, and which was guaranteed good because it cost $1,000 instead of $100.

February 5, 1961

SEISMOGRAPHY AND CENSUS-TAKING:
The Museum of Modern Art and the Whitney.

Two of New York's museums, the small Whitney Museum of American Art and the large Museum of Modern Art, are dedicated to the display and nurture of recent and contemporary work. Their functions, far from identical, overlap, with all the cards stacked against the Whitney. Not only is it small where the Museum of Modern Art is large; it is poor, and the Museum of Modern Art well off; the Museum of Modern Art is well-housed, while the Whitney is hamstrung by an unsympathetic building that, with its low ceilings and undefinably depressing proportions, manages to drain half the life out of anything exhibited in its galleries in spite of the best struggles of the curators. Even the Whitney's location in the Museum of Modern Art's back yard suggests that it is waiting for leftovers from the main table.

The Whitney's job is, or should be, to indicate the variety of expression in contemporary American painting. The Museum of Modern Art is free to forage internationally, America included. The range of American painting is wide but not all its expressions are spectacular. When it is spectacular the Museum of Modern Art makes the most of it; no other museum has ever dealt so skillfully with spectacular art spectacularly displayed under spectacular auspices. And since the Museum of Modern Art has become the most powerful influence on the formation of taste in this country, the public has come to identify the art that is most spectacular with the art that is best—a standard that makes many a fine and solid show at the Whitney seem second-rate.

The Museum of Modern Art indicates only a very small segment of the range of contemporary American painting. This is all right, since, in the first place, the Museum of Modern Art is not dedicated exclusively to American art and, in the second, it has set for itself the function of seismograph rather than of census taker. But its immense prestige, its flair for dramatic installation, its quick catches in the immediately contemporary game and its historical sense in reinterpreting a neglected subject, and its superb publications—all this has given the impression nationally and especially internationally that only the American painting it chooses (as seismograph) to exhibit is of any account.

The effect is vicious not because the Museum of Modern Art is vicious but because it has done its job so thoroughly and nobody else has done any other job. The Whitney's job is not to offer a rebuttal in opposition but to make its own explorations rather than to follow the cue of its neighbor. It has too often followed this cue as the fireworks have grown more brilliant, but this following has not been much more rewarding than the job of plugging away in its own direction. The Museum of Modern Art is quickest in dealing with the most arresting developments, and thus leaves the Whitney to record the latest shock-wave once-removed and weakened, along with the keeping of other records that are just as important but not shocking at all.

The Museum of Modern Art, however, is subject to one difficulty that the Whitney can spare itself. When you set yourself up as a seismographic observatory open to the public for a fee, the public expects to see an earthquake recorded every time it pays admission. Earthquakes are not that frequent, and neither are revolutions in art, not even today when the Museum of Modern Art's policy has led so many painters to force changes for change's sake, to strain at innovating rather than to plug away at perfecting.

Each Museum of Modern Art exhibition is expected to be a spectacular. No amount of explanation, in an exhibition catalogue, that the exhibition is presented as symptomatic can keep the public from believing that it is offered as the latest and biggest shakeup to date. Each annual show is expected to be the kind of thing that might be legitimate about once every ten years. This puts the museum in a spot where it offends one section of the public by appearing to sponsor any eccentricity. It thrills another section for the same reason, which should be even more painful for the curators and directors. In addition, the museum's tongue seems to hang out further every season as it meets the obligation to sustain the pace it has set.

But the Whitney is free to explore more slowly, more thoroughly and more quietly in a field geographically smaller but ideologically more extensive. It has the obligation to be more American and less New York-International. This doesn't mean, God forbid, a return to picturesque American subject matter and to flag waving, or a policy of underdogism. All it means is that there is a mass of important and inventive American painting that is neglected because it is not Museum of Modern Art fare, and that the Whitney can establish its own lead by finding this painting and showing it along with a proper proportion of the kind of thing that is better known because it has been turned into good box office.

If the Whitney hasn't money for such a program, its friends might ask themselves whether it is better to acquire expensive works by artists who are better represented next door, or to sponsor obscure painters who are working hard in less startling but surely just as valid directions.

Such a policy must result in many uneven shows and, of necessity, in scattered, contradictory and disharmonious shows. Kinds of painting judgeable as successful or unsuccessful by intelligent people familiar with established standards must be exhibited and the attendant risks taken. The Museum of Modern Art is less subject to risk because it deals with experiments in a field where standards are in such flux that the public has been brow-beaten to believe that it can hold no opinion of any consequence. To be howled at by reactionaries, which is the Museum of Modern Art's only risk with the public today, is no longer a risk, but an accepted accolade. To be derided by the avant-garde, which is the Whitney's risk in any honest survey, is still a risk indeed, since the appetite for novelty has made patrons suspicious of any contemporary work that does not bear the label of a currently popular ism.

There is, perhaps, no way out for the Whitney. "Exciting" having become the Museum of Modern Art's favorite adjective of esthetic description, excitement has become the public's esthetic yardstick. And we all know the stigma attached to the phrase "worth while."

September 18, 1960

THE LOUVRE:
A Love Letter.

New art museums are springing up all over the land. Perforce, they have a new look and often they serve new purposes. But frequently they leave a question as to whether the new look and the new purposes aren't achieved at the expense of what art museums are built to serve—in a word, art.

Rooms have gone out as space-flow has come in; walls have given way to movable partitions; paintings have been hung on rope nets like captured fish, or suspended from ceilings, and frames have become disfiguring inconveniences to be eliminated whenever possible. And you can find some contemporary art museums—handsome ones, too—of an architecture so clean, so spare and so clinically efficient that you may have difficulty in telling from the outside whether the inside is devoted to the stripping and examination of patients or paintings.

Efficiency is good, but none of it means a thing if a museum lacks one essential quality—if it is not a place where works of art, whether they were finished a thousand years ago or last week, can continue their lives and enrich ours. A work of art dies when it is displayed as a specimen. The first job of a museum is not to preserve a work of art as a corpse, but to sustain it as a living organism.

Perhaps the formula on which the clinic-museums are based is the only one appropriate to the conditions of what is always called "our time"—that scapegoat phrase by which we excuse so many of our half-achievements. But if the formula is any good, it should be flexible enough to accommodate values that are imperative to the functioning of the spirit. These are the values with which art is concerned, and for any architect or any museum director who has forgotten what they are, a visit to the Louvre should serve as a chastening refresher course in what an art museum should be, even if it cannot be, like the Louvre, the greatest one in the world.

Just what is this Louvre, and what quality does it have that has made the word "Louvre" less the designation of a place than a symbol in men's minds?

During the tourist season this year, from April through September, between 900,000 and 1,000,000 people will have tromped, sauntered, plodded, trotted, ambled, strolled or been wheeled through the Louvre's galleries. People accustomed to taking taxis to lunch will irrationally hope to cover the whole museum—the equivalent of walking down Fifth Avenue from Ninetieth Street to the far side of Washington Square—to see the paintings, and back again to cover the mileage of tapestries, sculpture, furniture and the like. This doesn't count ceilings, and, in the Louvre, these are liberally decorated with paintings ranging from the best to the most routine productions of great, near-great, once-great and never-great artists who from time to time have been commissioned to do them.

The question *"Où est la Mona Lisa?"* will be asked tens of thousands of times in accents ranging from English, German, Italian, Spanish, Chinese, Japanese and Hindustani to French Provincial. From 10 A.M., when the museum opens, to 5 P.M., when it closes, the Venus de Milo will be located by ear from distant points, the vortex of a great, swelling roar, compounded of the shuffling of approaching and departing feet and punctuated by cries of recognition laced with the explanatory multilingual drone of conducted tours.

The first-time unguided visitors who enter with the intention of looking at every object in the place may never get as far as the main staircase, at the top of which the Nike of Samothrace—the "Winged Victory"—is magnificently installed. Old-timers will give her a passing salute as they head directly for a favorite area, such as the Roman sculpture galleries, which are cool and relatively quiet, or a certain room of Persian antiquities, which has a good view of the Louvre-Tuileries-Concorde-Elysées-Arc de Triomphe axis and is occupied only by a guard who, over the decades, has lost the power of speech. But to find a bench to sit on, it may be necessary to go as far as the Ancient Near East rooms, which are seldom frequented, and then mostly by archaeologists.

Small bands of returning explorers, ready to weep from that combination of sore feet and brain fag known as museum fatigue, follow series of signs promising *"Sortie,"* originating at the easternmost dead end of the palace labyrinth and leading upstairs, downstairs, and through subterranean passageways to an exit several city blocks from the one they are hunting. Even habitués get lost sometimes, and in their wanderings continue to find nooks and crannies that have escaped them, with the treasures therein—for instance, in the decorative arts wing, an unexpected circular alcove about fifteen feet in diameter crammed with sculptures by Houdon, where a nude nymph in the center is regarded by a ring of exceptionally alert-looking portrait busts of eighteenth-century dignitaries, including Washington, Franklin and Jefferson.

At a guess, 90 per cent of the summer visitors to the Louvre are performing a duty or, at best, are hoping that through voluntary exposure they will absorb a little culture by osmosis. Their chances of doing so in the Louvre are better than they are anywhere else, although what takes place in the Louvre takes place to some degree in every city where tourists, and residents, go to museums.

The Uffizi in Florence, by comparison with the Louvre, is a kind of local historical society on a sublime scale. The Prado in Madrid is a series of incomparable one-man shows by Velasquez, El Greco, Goya and visiting Italians and Flemings. The German museums are superb textbooks of art history. London's National Gallery is an impressive souvenir of cool aristocratic taste. And New York's Metropolitan demonstrates how far acumen, industry and money can carry you in a field even if you begin after 99 per cent of the cream has been skimmed off and stashed away elsewhere.

These are great collections, yet we think of them first of all as collections. But the Louvre is the Louvre—a collection, a palace, a concept and a symbol. It nourishes and sustains by something beyond the inexhaustible richness of its treasure. When we say "Louvre," we think of the whole thing, the whole physical complex of palace and objects plus the abstract concept of a combined depository and well-spring of Western culture, of art as the ultimate and enduring and continuing expression of man's thought.

As for the palace of the Louvre, it was not originally meant to be a public exhibition building, but became one by degrees, and just about everything is wrong with it by contemporary aseptic and functional standards of what an art museum should be. The origins of the word "Louvre" are unknown, although one dubious explanation connects it with *louveterie,* which could be a lodge or fortress as a center for wolf hunts. There was certainly a fort on the site in 1204.

The present building dates from the time of Francis I to 1902. Its halls are wasteful of space in the grand manner, and sullenly inflexible. It is fantastically expensive to maintain and virtually impossible to guard properly. It is hard to get around in. Its elaborate décor ranges through a dozen historical and pseudo-historical periods and should be distractingly out of harmony with half the works on display. About the only good thing you can say for the Louvre as a place to show pictures is that it is perfect. To say anything else is to say that certain pockmarks on Mount Everest disqualify it in its own category.

Furthermore, until recently ("recently" for the Louvre means the last forty or fifty years, and "soon" means the next forty or fifty), the Louvre was not only the greatest museum in the world but also the worst run. The national treasures were crowded into it for safekeeping and the public was admitted to look at them, and that was that. (It was, of course, a lot.) Nobody was quite sure where anything was; galleries would be closed for weeks and nobody would know why; outside of protecting the works of art from the weather, little effort was made toward their preservation and repair.

For twenty years or so, the Louvre has been refurbishing itself, hanging pictures so that they are not shouldered on all four sides by others, and building small rooms inside big ones to display small pictures, for instance. But a few diehards have been known to grumble about these supposed improvements, like loving husbands who preferred their wives' old faces to the new ones requisitioned from the surgeon.

And these dissenters have a point, in that the wonder and

glory of the Louvre is the sense of tradition, a feeling of continuing life that is exactly the opposite of the high-class-merchandise display or the preservation-in-a-vacuum concepts that lately have made American museums the models for new European ones and quite possibly the spiritual executioners of the museum idea as it developed originally in France.

But to these menaces the Louvre is immune, even when it makes concessions to them. In spite of current reforms, there is still an engagingly *dégagé* air to much that goes on in the place. It has an unconquerable life of its own that resists every effort to subject it to current disciplinary vogues. It is simply too big and too various to be run except on a semi-improvisational basis.

An exhibition announced for a certain date may open a month earlier or a month later, and only fools ask why. It is just the way things work out. This is not the result of indifference or insouciance on the part of the administration, but of a certain practicality based on the knowledge that when a Louvre exhibition does materialize, it is going to be so absolutely bang-up that minor details, such as when and for how long, are beside the point.

The same beguiling informality in the face of magnificence is apparent in the museum's daily program. A visitor who happened to see the Louvre's night guards getting ready to go on duty at closing time reports that each was issued a mammoth ancient key and a small, battered gooseneck reading lamp (God knows what the wiring in the Louvre is like) while one of the group also picked up what was apparently a communal hot plate. The whole thing suggested the preliminaries of a midnight fudge party in a dormitory rather than a police action in a museum.

Considering the importance of their positions, the direc-

torial and curatorial staff of the Louvre are similarly informal. American curators glow about their collections. The
curators of the Louvre are not exactly casual about their
trusts, but neither are they euphoric. It is perfectly natural,
they feel, that these treasures should be where they are,
a logical consequence of several centuries of world history.
Significantly, the American attitude implies with every proud
burble that it is unnatural for a really fine painting by an
old master to be on this side of the water.

It may, indeed, be unnatural. The pictures in the Louvre
are a heritage and a continuation of the cultural interplay
of the days when French royalty and aristocrats and other
patrons either commissioned them or imported them or stole
them or acquired them half by accident; they are something
other than the artificial, high-priced, prestige symbols that
they are in America. After the Revolution, the great collections were simply appropriated by the new state, for the
people.

To the extent that American culture is tied to that of
Europe, we can claim a legitimate right to purchase our
portion of evidence of the past, but by the standards that
make the Louvre the greatest museum in the world, the
standards of history, of tradition and what we might call
"natural acquisition," American avidity for bought culture
has just a touch of *mauvais goût*.

And, when you come down to it, some of our new museum
buildings and most of our new display techniques support
this unhappy thought. Cold and dramatic at the same time,
they imply that we are less interested in enjoying works of
art than in owning and displaying them, and putting them
to use as means toward the end of increasing our culture
status.

The attitude is exaggerated, if anything, in the case of modern art, even when a painting is a contemporary American one to which we have every right in the world. A community may point with pride to its Pollock (a Pollock costs up to $100,000) even while it observes it with displeasure.

When it comes to observing with pleasure, there is no place in the world where this pleasure is so complete, so rich, so inexhaustible, so natural and so loving as at the Louvre. This is what makes the Louvre the great comfort and the great reassurance for all men who think that the game, during the last few thousand years, has been worth the candle.

The architectural design and the directorial programs of the clinic-museum offer no such reassurance. Obviously, we cannot have little Louvres in city after city, but we can learn from the Louvre that while a museum may be a place for the exhibition, the study and the preservation of works of art, it should not be first of all a showcase, a laboratory or a cold-storage plant. It should be, first of all, a fitting habitation.

September 4, 1960

WRIGHT VERSUS PAINTING:
The Guggenheim Museum.

The Solomon R. Guggenheim Museum, open to the public as of this afternoon, is a war between architecture and painting in which both come out badly maimed. The Pyrrhic victory belongs to the architecture, or to the shade of the architect, the late Frank Lloyd Wright, over the museum's director, James Johnson Sweeney, who was faced with the problem of adapting an abstract architectural composition to its function as an exhibition gallery. But Mr. Wright's snail-curl balcony, climbing in circles from ground level to dome level around a great core of space, was an invincible opponent.

At so important an event as the opening of this building and the exhibition in it, graceful courtesies belong in dedicatory speeches. But a critique of the museum must be as objective as possible, unaffected by the excitement of the occasion or by gratitude for the philanthropy that brings an important monument to the city to house an increasingly important collection.

As the big building rose at 1071 Fifth Avenue, at Eighty-eighth Street, so many tales circulated about difficulties encountered in making it into a usable museum, and about desperate expedients to make it work, that the whole affair began to sound like a salvage operation. Ignoring these stories in the light of the completed job, and leaving operational difficulties to be dealt with behind the scenes, what does the public see?

There are plenty of scars to show that Mr. Sweeney has put up a game and ingenious fight against an impossible scheme. Mr. Wright was not too fond of painting, believing that its only legitimate function was that of an adjunct to architecture. If he had deliberately designed an interior to annihilate painting as an expressive art, and to reduce it to an architectural accessory, he could not have done much better. It takes effort and concentration to savor the pictures

for themselves, even though Mr. Wright's original scheme
for their hanging has been modified to their advantage.

Mr. Wright made a moderately ambiguous statement on
the lighting he visualized for the paintings that line the outside wall of his snail-curve. (The inside curve drops off into
the vast central pit, from which one is protected by a rather
frighteningly low parapet.) Mr. Wright objected to the "constant flood of artificial light" in which, according to opinions
other than his, pictures are best displayed. He said that "the
charm of any work of art, either of painting, sculpture or
architecture, is to be seen in normal, naturally changing
light." Thus on gray days, Mr. Wright believed, the pictures
should go dim along with the rest of the interior, or on bright
days brighten with it, and so on, in spite of some assistance
from artificial sources.

Regarding pictures as part of an architectural whole, fine.
Regarding pictures as something one comes to a museum to
see, terrible, if the sun is not out.

The lighting has been redesigned to maintain a steady
illumination for the benefit of the pictures. The paintings
project from the wall on long metal arms attached to the
centers of their backs (Mr. Sweeney's idea, not Mr. Wright's)
seeming to float in space, dramatically. They are thus beautifully revealed, but at the expense of the total architectural
harmony. They occupy their space so uncomfortably, like
intruders, that their clear revelation loses much of its point.
One comes again and again to the conclusion that the solution is a tragic compromise, yet that no better compromise
could be found.

In addition, the snail-curl is a kind of strait jacket for the
visitor. No wandering back and forth from one favorite picture to another. No going from room to room through con-

venient doors. One is inexorably led from picture to picture
and from level to level along the spiral, with only an occasional lucky assist when the elevator is in the right spot.

. Finally there is the sheer geometrical implacability of a
spiral. By its slant, its occasional subtle flattenings, its odd
curves and its curious junctures with partitions, the spiral
creates to a small but very bothersome degree the giddiness
of the fun house in amusement parks where everything is
built in a skewed perspective so that one tumbles and falls.

Progression through the spiral makes one dizzy, not from
the slow circular movement, but from the verticals that are
not quite vertical, the horizontals that are not quite horizontal, the right angles that are not quite right. The pictures
seem to hang askew, seen from one point, and to hang askew
in the opposite direction seen from another. And those seen
from across the central void, looking up or down, are unpleasantly bisected, with only a top or bottom showing.

The new museum is frequently compared to the Pantheon
in Rome, sometimes to Hagia Sophia, in Istanbul, both also
architectural designs of space surmounted by domes and illuminated from them. Those elaborately ornamented buildings are harmonious entities because ornament and architecture are harmonious.

Stripped of its pictures, existing solely as a design, Mr.
Wright's building might be a third in the trio. But unfor-
tunately the pictures disfigure the building and the building
disfigures the pictures, and in honesty, for this writer at any
rate, there is no point in pretending anything else.

October 21, 1959

FROM SALON TO CELLAR:
Nineteenth Century Academic Painting.

A kind of convection current operates along the walls of museums, particularly in America, by which pictures move from location to location over the years according to the warmth or chilliness of critical favor. If a speeded-up film could be made of this process over the past several decades, similar to those in which we see flowers coming into bud, blossoming, and dropping their petals all in a matter of seconds, what a heaving and jostling we should see! But among the minor fluctuating movements, we could follow one group of pictures in a great downward plunge from places of honor into the limbo of basement storage, where they have remained as sedimental refuse to be avoided as if poisonous. These are the popular favorites of the nineteenth century, the French Salon paintings and their equivalent types elsewhere in Europe and in England—the paintings that were riding high, and priced high, while impressionism was a scandal and impressionist paintings could be bought for the price of a good Salon frame.

No tables have ever turned more completely. But lately there has been a stirring within the depths, a quiet and half-surreptitious upward seepage of Salon painting from basement into backstair halls, into odds and ends of spaces not much visited, and occasionally even into the exhibition galleries proper. It is increasingly possible to see not only Cézanne, whom everybody knows, but also his contemporary Gérôme whom everybody has forgotten although he was so well thought of during his lifetime that his objections to impressionism (he called it "filth" which only a "great moral slackening" could make acceptable) helped keep some extremely good pictures, including Cézanne's, out of the Louvre. It is possible also to see Renoir, whom everybody loves, on one wall and Bouguereau, whom everybody used to love, on another nearby. It is not yet safe to suggest that Renoir at his worst and Bouguereau at his best may have something in common, but in all probability someone is going to open that sluice gate before long.

At present the safe attitude toward Salon painting is one of amused condescension. Even this is a step upward for the outcasts: horror and revulsion were obligatory only a few years ago. In the story of modern—that is, latter nineteenth- and early twentieth-century—art, the Salon painters have been presented as the Bad Guys and the impressionists, whom indeed they persecuted, as the Good Guys. But the defeat of the villains has been complete enough to satisfy even their bitterest enemies. Just why the undeniable faults and the possible virtues of Salon painting have been so juggled about takes a little explaining.

The Salon originated as an official exhibition in which accredited painters could present their work, summarize their theories, and introduce their protégés, usually by means of large demonstration pictures. The importance of the Salon in France, a country where art has always been part of the fabric of national life and where, until recently, the exhibition of a picture could affect the prestige of the government, is hard to understand in a country where the most nearly comparable institution is the Automobile Show, and where the commercial dealer has taken over the function of middleman between artist and public. The Salon still exists, in an abject and pointless way, but effectively it died of giantism in the nineteenth century.

Around a quarter of a million paintings must have been given official exhibition in France between 1800 and 1900, and as many more presented for exhibition but rejected by the juries. Most of them were, of necessity, bad or at best inconsequential, since there simply are not enough good painters working at any time to produce that many good pictures anywhere, not even in France. Ready to drop of its own weight, the Salon was given the *coup de grâce* by its own abuses. It became not only the annual testing ground for new talent and the prancing ground for established talent, but also the torture chamber for any exceptional picture that happened to get in for one reason or another, as Manet's "Olympia" did in 1865.

The Salon juries were dominated by the pedants of the French Academy, an institution whose history in the nineteenth century is appalling, whose practices were loathed by every artist and intellectual of much perception, and whose chairs continued to be coveted beyond all other honors nevertheless. As one of the five branches of the Institute of France, the Academy of Fine Arts was nominally dedicated to the recognition of French genius and the fostering of the highest achievements in art. In practice the Academy became a closed circle of conventional talents, of men skilled equally in the manipulation of trite formulas for painting and the manipulation of advantageous personal contacts. The situation was deplorable, but it was also inevitable. Mediocrity rather than villainy accounted for the academic persecution of painters who are now recognized as the great ones of the century; the academicians sincerely believed that they were defending the purity and sanity of art against the assaults of boors and madmen.

Genius being, by definition, original, its manifestations could hardly be perceived by a group of men in positions of entrenched privilege whose election to the Academy was part of the assumption that the formulas for great art had been crystallized once and for all. Delacroix, who was finally elected to the Academy when he was old, sick, and tired, and who continued to be snubbed by its officials even after election, once said that an academician taught beauty as one teaches arithmetic. The Salons were made up of thousands of these exercises in addition and subtraction, hung frame to frame from floor to ceiling in vast halls through which the public thronged to admire or to deride, taking their cue from the critics—and to buy.

Painting became merchandise and the Salon became a gigantic salesroom. A painter who couldn't manage to get into it had little chance of selling his pictures for a decent price, or of placing them with a dealer, or even of getting them into another spot where many people were likely to see them. The Salon took on the nature of a life-and-death arena for the painter because he had become dependent upon a new kind of buyer. Before the nineteenth century the artist worked for small and cultivated groups of patrons, but this class had its head chopped off in the French Revolution. As the century coalesced into the great age of the common man, the painter had to find his living in the open market by appealing to an esthetically ignorant public on other than esthetic grounds. An ecstatic love affair developed between the affluent purchaser with mediocre taste and the skilled painter of mediocre conceptions. And the Salon was their trysting place.

Two considerations above all others attracted buyers. The first was slick technique, which made of the painter a kind of stunt man: the technical level of Salon painting was very high. The second was anecdotal interest. A painting had first of all to be an illustration, and a painter could base a long and successful career on a single anecdotal gimmick. The painter Vibert, for instance, who was a superb technician, devoted his talent to anecdote after anecdote after anecdote showing Roman cardinals as lovable old codgers in humorously undignified situations, or depicting young priests being naïvely taken aback by the worldly pranks of their parishioners. More "serious" painters inflated their anecdotes with sentimental moralizing and intellectual pretension. The typical Salon painting flattered the prospective purchaser by assuring him that his favorable response was the result of his moral probity, his intellectual acumen, and his cultural elevation.

Pictures like Gérôme's "Pygmalion and Galatea" filled the bill on every score. The anecdote was ready-made, since the Pygmalion story has always been a good one. And as presented with all its pre-Shavian classical trappings, it also flattered the observer by assuming his familiarity with classical legend. This was culture. The fair lady, being naked for legitimate reasons, could be legitimately ogled. This was a pleasure. And Gérôme's impeccable technique was turned to a ravishing novelty effect: the statue-woman grades from luscious pink, where she has come to life (and has already started to work) down to pure white, where she is still marble. This was where the art came in, and what more could you ask? Daumier's hilarious burlesque of the subject suggests a disconcerting answer—yet a public with access to this cartoon continued to take Gérôme seriously.

Armies of nudes swarmed across the Salon walls, pretty girls without a stitch on but elaborately disguised by titles. A bourgeois society obsessed with the surface observance of a moral code unsympathetic to the display of the body found the most delicious release in artistic subterfuge. The Emperor Napoleon III himself bought Cabanel's provocative "Birth of Venus" out of the Salon of 1863, yet in 1865 Manet's "Olympia" was a scandal for its "indecency." Cabanel's Folies-Bergère beauty suggests one thing and one thing alone: even the official critics found her daringly "wanton." But since she was a Venus conventionally and very skillfully painted by a ranking academician, everything was all right. The culture more than made up for the wantonness, and the lines of the picture were found to be "of great purity," which helped. But Manet's masterpiece was compared to "high" game and the people who gathered around it, to morbid curiosity seekers in a morgue. This latter comparison was not far from wrong, since they had come to see a "dirty" picture, the critics having given this label to "Olympia" because the model was boldly and objectively painted as a Parisian courtesan, unabashed. Honesty was always a dangerous policy in the Salon.

The nude had been a standard test piece for centuries, but since art for art's sake did not interest the Salon public, and since the nude for the sake of the nude was morally suspect, the Salon painters invented a hundred ways to involve nudes or semi-nudes in acceptable anecdotal situations. Psychiatrists should have no trouble explaining why these females got into so many painted difficulties. They were always being sold into slavery while prospective buyers subjected them to such indignities as examining their teeth. They were often put to the torture—lashed to stakes and the like—and they languished in prisons on heaps of straw while coarse guards stood by indifferently. They couldn't so much as disrobe for a quick dip in a woodland pool without being taken by surprise. Naturally, they resented all this, and their expressions of outraged modesty allowed the observers in the Salon to combine perfectly normal sympathy for the poor things with equally normal but less open response to their charms. Every figure in history who could conceivably be shown undraped or partially undraped was represented time and again. Then there were the nymphs, the bacchantes, and the other lively creatures who by tradition could not only go naked but could be sportive about the whole thing because, like Venus, they had been playing the culture circuit since ancient times.

Children were almost as popular as nudes, and it was even easier to find things for them to do. Without question, the Salon produced in its simpering, mincing pictures of childhood the most offensively coy images in the history of painting. Animals were often painted in much the same vein, self-consciously engaged in being cute. At other times they were reproduced objectively enough, going about their normal occupations of grazing or just standing still. Cows and sheep held an unreasonable fascination for Salon painters and their public, explainable, possibly, as urban man's nostalgic recollection of a more tranquil pastoral age. The cow in the living room became a familiar phenomenon, and a painter's knowledge of bovine anatomy was commented on as seriously as other painters' knowledge of the human figure.

Rosa Bonheur in France and Sir Edwin Landseer in England were the most conspicuous animal painters. Landseer could give a stag at eve all the pompous air of an eminent clubman, and his dogs were noted for their sensitive intelligence and subtle emotional responses. Landseer pushed his

<small>Bouguereau:</small> *NYMPHS AND SATYR*, 1873. 101¾″ x 71″. Oil on canvas. Courtesy of the Sterling and Francine Clark Art Institute, Williamstown, Massachusetts.

special variation of the pathetic fallacy to new limits; his animals ran an emotional gamut as wide as that of the French nudes. He was not so much a painter as he was the Sarah Bernhardt of taxidermy.

To categorize pictures of the Salon type, whether French, German, English, or of any other country, we would have to list the history pictures, the picturesque landscapes, the picturesque interiors, the travelogue pictures—usually of the Near East, the jolly peasants, the noble peasants, the pert old ladies, the melancholy old ladies, the fashionable portraits, the religious pictures, the allegories, and the imitations of every old master then in favor. One could belabor each of these types in turn, but in the end we would come down to the same conclusion: that the rank and file of Salon painting was skillfully trite, obvious, and vulgar.

So much for that. It is a harsh judgment, but now the usual one on a kind of painting that offers a field day for gibes. It is helpless in its awfulness, exposed in all its shortcomings, unpardonable in its sentimentality in a day when "sentimental" is a more damning word than "obscene." Yet, if Gérôme is ludicrous in "Pygmalion and Galatea" and in nine-tenths of the rest of his work, and merely dull in nine-tenths of the remaining fraction, occasionally he paints an anecdote like "Duel After the Masquerade," which is so nicely patterned, so succinct in its narrative, and so unexpected in the nature of the narrative, that only a fanatic modernist can refuse to recognize its virtues. And if most Salon children are offensive brats, a few of them have great charm. Salon painting was based on a precise imitation of nature, in spite of all the prettying-up and the artificial posing. When children were painted directly, sympathetically, and without all the rigmarole that turned them into bad actors on amateur night, they could be attractive subjects for a kind of painting that was expert in the presentation of externals. And if Landseer's animals are usually mawkish, he also painted "Blackcock," a harmony in whites, tans, and greys with a spot of red, in pigment so opulently weighted that the picture would do credit to Courbet. The good Landseers, isolated from the infection of the typical mass of his work, suggest that here was one of the best minor painters of his century, instead of one of the laughable worst.

There is gold in the storerooms; it need only be panned out. As a random example, there is Eduard Charlemont, an Austrian who was born in 1848 and died in 1906, who apparently had a moderate success during his lifetime but whose name, surely, would not be familiar to one out of fifty or a hundred curators of painting or historians and teachers of art. There is not much reason why it should be. He was in no way an innovator, and he probably painted large numbers of dull pictures. But his "Moorish Chief," which has been pulled out of storage in Philadelphia and is the kind of picture that might as easily have been found in a secondhand shop or in the random stock of an unselective dealer, is a beautiful piece of work, expertly painted, richly colored, superbly drawn, and neatly joined. These satisfactions are offered for themselves and can be enjoyed for themselves: the subject, a conventional bit of orientalism, is only a peg upon which to hang them and is unobtrusive because it is not forced into a pretense of more depth than it has.

Charlemont takes little more interest in his model as a Moorish chieftain than the cubists took in the violins, tables, and compotes that served them as points of departure for technical exercises. But his exercise is at least as legitimate,

EDUARD CHARLEMONT: *MOORISH CHIEF*, 1878. 58⅛″ x 38½″. Oil on wood. Courtesy of the John G. Johnson Collection, Philadelphia.

in many ways more difficult, and at the moment not a bit more threadbare, than exercises in abstraction; it is just that the abstract virtues of figurative painting are assumed not to exist by critics and artists who cannot see beyond their noses because these have for so long been pressed against nonfigurative canvases. It is easy to imagine Picasso or, even more, Matisse responding to the merits of "Moorish Chief"; it is impossible to imagine the little Picassos and the little Matisses doing so, since they are committed to a blanket rejection of representational painting unless it bears the tag of a great name. With a falsified label (say, Delacroix, 1824), "Moorish Chief" would be sensational not only as an important picture historically, which it is not, but also as a superb piece of painting, which it is.

There are several good arguments in favor of ending the exile of Salon painting. The most objective one is that as part of the context of nineteenth-century art it has been neglected. Historians always weight the scale, but good ones do not pretend that certain things did not happen just because they don't approve of them. Regarding himself as an arbiter of taste, a museum curator of painting may decide for himself what he wants to hang (and lay himself wide open to the delighted laughter of the next generation); but regarding himself as the caretaker of man's long pictorial record of himself, the curator might try for a more representative display of that record than he has done recently in the case of nineteenth-century painting.

Outside the museums there are other reasons for lifting the ban. With Cézannes selling for half a million (which is not too much for a Cézanne, but is more than most of us can afford) and "Moorish Chief" selling for a few hundred dollars, the delight of owning a good painting is likely to lead collectors (and dealers) into new fields. In addition, that good old Pendulum of Time (a fine title for a Salon allegory) is still swinging, and a reversion to realism away from abstraction, prophesied by some critics wishfully and by others fearfully, may lead to new sympathies.

But if the revival really gets under way, it could snowball for a reason that not many people can accept without dismay: Salon painting still appeals to a large section of the public for exactly the same reasons, alas, that it appealed a hundred years ago when it was fresh off the easels.

Horizon, March, 1960

APPENDIX:
The Embattled Critic

The following letter attacking me as art critic of *The New York Times* was printed on the art page on Sunday, February 26, 1961, without comment. It brought responses from more than 600 readers, with about 550 of them supporting me—not all of these, however, for the right reasons from my point of view.

On the two subsequent Sundays, March 5 and 12, 1961, *The Times* printed fifty-two letters, pro and con, as a debate. In spite of their personal tone, which cannot be edited out, these letters can be read as an informal discussion of a critic's function and position today, and the selection given here, based on that made by *The Times*, is offered as such.

There are many more pro than con letters, partly to observe the proportionate relation of the letters that came in, but largely because the con letters did little but repeat the accusations made in the original letter. Some of the letters have been expanded to include portions of the originals that were edited out for reasons of space when published in *The Times*. There are a couple of changes in the titles of the signatories of the original letter, in one case at the request of the signatory, in another at the request of the institution with which he is connected.

The original letter:

To THE NEW YORK TIMES:

Reading Mr. John Canaday's columns on contemporary art, we regard as offensive his consistent practice of going beyond discussion of exhibitions in order to impute to living artists en masse, as well as to critics, collectors and scholars of present-day American art, dishonorable motives, those of cheats, greedy lackeys or senseless dupes.

Here are some instances:

Sept. 20, 1959: "* * * a situation built on fraud at worst and gullibility at best has produced a school of such prolix mediocrity * * *"

July 24, 1960: "The chaotic, haphazard and bizarre nature of modern art is easily explained: The painter finally settles for whatever satisfaction may be involved in working not as an independent member of a society that needs him, but as a retainer for a small group of people who as a profession or as a hobby are interested in the game of comparing one mutation with another."

Sept. 6, 1959: "But as for the freaks, the charlatans and the misled who surround this handful of serious and talented artists, let us admit at least that the nature of abstract expressionism allows exceptional tolerance for incompetence and deception."

"In the meanwhile, critics and educators have been hoist with their own petard, sold down the river. We have been had."

Sept. 11, 1960: "* * * for a decade the bulk of abstract art in America has followed that course of least resistance and quickest profit."

"There is not a dealer in town, nor a collector, nor a painter hoping to hang in the Museum of Modern Art who doesn't study each of Mr. Barr's syllables in an effort to deduce what he should offer for sale, what he should buy, or what he should paint * * *"

Oct. 23, 1960: "* * * brainwashing * * * goes on in universities and museums."

Mr. Canaday is entitled, of course, to the freedom of his

opinions regarding works of art. We submit, however, that his terminology of insults is scarcely adequate to describe emerging art works and tendencies, and we scorn this waging of a polemical campaign under the guise of topical reporting.

If Mr. Canaday has a political or social or esthetic "position" or philosophy, let him state what it is and openly promote his aims. Every style and movement in art history contains examples of work by imitative or uninterested artists. To keep referring to these in order to impugn the whole, instead of attempting to deal seriously with the work of the movement, is the activity not of a critic but of an agitator.

JAMES S. ACKERMAN, Professor of Fine Arts, Harvard University.

WILLIAM BARRETT, Professor of Philosophy, N. Y. U.

DONALD BLINKEN, Collector.

WALTER BAREISS, Collector.

BERNARD BRODSKY, M.D., Collector.

JAMES BROOKS, Painter.

JOHN CAGE, Composer.

BERNARD CHAET, Associate Professor of Painting, School of Art and Architecture, Yale University.

HOWARD CONANT, Chairman, Dept. of Art Education, N. Y. U.

STUART DAVIS, Painter.

EDWIN DENBY, Writer.

HENRY EPSTEIN, Collector.

JOHN FERREN, Painter.

ALFRED FRANKFURTER, Editor & President, "Art News."

PERCIVAL GOODMAN, Architect, F.A.I.A.

ADOLPH GOTTLIEB, Painter.

JACK M. GREENBAUM, Collector.

Mr. & Mrs. I. Harold Grossman, Collectors.

David Hare, Sculptor.

Ben Heller, Collector.

Thomas B. Hess, Executive Editor, "Art News."

Hans Hofmann, Painter.

Sam Hunter, Director, Rose Art Museum, Brandeis University.

Kenneth Koch, Writer.

Willem de Kooning, Painter.

Stanley Kunitz, Poet.

Kermit Lansner, Writer.

Boris Leavitt, Collector.

Erle Loran, Painter and Teacher.

Arnold H. Maremont, Collector, Chicago.

Robert Motherwell, Painter.

E. A. Navaretta, Poet and Critic.

Albert H. Newman, Collector.

Barnett Newman, Painter.

Raymond Parker, Painter.

Phillip Pavia, Sculptor, Editor, "It Is."

Gifford Phillips, Collector, Publisher, "Frontier Magazine."

William Phillips, Editor, "Partisan Review."

Fairfield Porter, Art Critic, "The Nation."

David A. Prager, Collector.

Harold Rosenberg, Writer.

Robert Rosenblum, Assistant Professor, Dept. of Art & Archaeology, Princeton University.

Barney Rossett, Publisher, Grove Press.

Irving Sandler, Writer and Critic.

Kenneth B. Sawyer, Art Critic, Baltimore Sun.

David Smith, Sculptor.

WHITNEY S. STODDARD, Professor of Art.

MEYER SCHAPIRO, Professor, Dept. of Art History and Archaeology, Columbia University.

PAUL WEISS, Professor of Philosophy, Yale University.

Some replies:

TO THE EDITOR:

If I were your critic John Canaday, I would consider as a compliment the letter to The New York Times printed in last Sunday's issue. By and large, the signers of the letter constitute the "party" and their letter the "line" which could reasonably be expected as a result of Mr. Canaday's refreshing departure from the current critical rut which offers itself but fails to pass as art criticism.

The weakness of the letter writers is found within the terms of their letter itself. The essence of the signers' compliment is their scorn of Canaday's "waging of a polemical campaign under the guise of topical reporting." That is really putting the rabbit into the hat for the sole purpose of taking it out again. Whoever suggested that it is The Times' critic's function to do "topical reporting," that his writing is done under such guise, or that any non-member of the "party" would settle for mere topical reporting in the art columns of your paper?

The letter goes on to suggest that "if Mr. Canaday has a * * * position or philosophy, let him state what it is and openly promote his aims." He seems to have made his statement clearly and vigorously enough to have gotten under the

skins of the letter writers and to have been accused of waging a "polemical campaign." In their opening paragraph they
themselves summarize his statement and "position" as im-
puting "to living artists en masse, as well as to critics, collectors and scholars of present-day American art, dishonest
motives, those of cheats, greedy lackeys or senseless dupes."
What they are really complaining of, therefore, is not that
he has failed to clarify his statement and position but that
they do not like the statement he has made and the position
he has taken. They are really objecting to criticism adverse
to their views and interests.

Perhaps the most ironic aspect of the letter is that it in-
cludes among its signers Alfred Frankfurter and Thomas B.
Hess, the editor and executive editor respectively of Art News.
In the first place, whatever perfection may be lacking in Mr.
Canaday's writing and criticism, it never descends to the
level of linguistic drivel which appears regularly in every
issue of Art News. (Examples will be supplied on request.)
And secondly, the letter suggested that Mr. Canaday's writing "is the activity not of a critic but of an agitator." Mr.
Hess's editorials in Art News, attacking Mr. Canaday, com-
plained that Mr. Canaday lacks "enthusiasm" and emotional
involvement with modern art, and the complaint now is that
he is an agitator. Apparently, "enthusiasm" and involvement
are laudable only if they are one-sided.

Finally, a different kind of comment about Mr. Canaday
and his articles. I don't always agree with him—and I
wouldn't like it if I did. The important thing is that he
has the courage to take an unfashionably moderate position in a time when the avant-garde has become more academic than any academy and when it has become treason to

do anything less than accept all of its products as master work.

Ralph F. Colin.

New York.

The list of artists, educators and art collectors who signed a letter of protest against Mr. Canaday's articles is an imposing one. Hitherto these distinguished gentlemen have represented the kind of liberal thought and tolerant action which championed the expression of dissenting opinion. It is thus sad to me, who have also devoted my energy and thought to abstract art, to read of these fellow artists and admired connoisseurs campaigning vindictively against a man of integrity and intelligence who dares to express an unfashionable opinion. . . .

Mr. Canaday's disagreement with a lot of the ideas which impel the current avant-garde is responsible for the opposition to his writing. The whimpering of this group, which has for many years dominated the art world, is not worthy of its achievements. Can these men brook no inquiry into the sources of their ideas, no investigation of their purposes, no opposition to some of their conclusions?

As an abstract painter, I have read Mr. Canaday's criticism with considerable attention. Even though I may agree with only half of what he writes, I am delighted to read criticism which is founded on knowledge, constructed with thought and expressed in clear English. The very fact that I do not always agree with Mr. Canaday is one I find stimulating and worthwhile. It helps me to question my own ideas, to verify or reject them; this is a healthy and useful process.

If Mr. Canaday has the courage to search for ideals and

the intellect to illuminate his search, we, his readers, ought to measure up to his challenge. I am sure he would be the first one to welcome constructive and intelligible opposition, for it would be directed to the same aim he has: an attempt better to understand the relationship of contemporary life and art. The energies of the formidable group whose letter has prompted mine could well be devoted to this kind of understanding rather than to crying "foul" or "out of bounds" when a critic re-examines the values of a decade.

CLEVE GRAY.

Cornwall Bridge, Conn.

The letter is directed against the whole profession of art criticism. Its contents are directed to cripple a specific critic and any other critic honestly interested in informing an interested public.

To take Mr. Canaday apart for pointing out the existence of charlatans, frauds, fakes and mountebanks in art is to deny all history and to place art in a position unique among all professions that involve money and prestige. Every signer of the letter must be aware of this fact. To threaten Mr. Canaday with unnamed consequences if he does not wholeheartedly subscribe to the "movement" is so reminiscent of the methods of the academies of a century ago and of the politics of the Axis countries in the Nineteen Thirties that the letter is, to put it mildly, a dangerous anachronism.

CHARLES H. MORGAN.

Amherst, Mass.

It seems curious that in an age in which basic freedoms are at issue over much of the world, a critic should be attacked for expressing opinions with which not all of us are in accord.

RICHARD B. K. McLANATHAN.

Utica, N. Y.

A scalping party is not conducive to enlightenment. This affair saddens us particularly when we note respected faculty names from Yale and Columbia who we felt would never be part of a lynch crowd.

LAURI J. ANDERSON, D. D.

New York.

Since their charges won't quite stick, and since they make no attempt whatever to refute Mr. Canaday's serious criticism of their movement, one is forced to conclude that the cardinal complaint of the signatories of the letter attacking John Canaday is not against what he says, so much as the fact that he says it in a newspaper which reaches a far wider audience than anything they have access to through such publications as Art News and It Is.

Mr. Canaday is not engaged in "topical reporting," but in art criticism which happens to have a news peg; just as were George Bernard Shaw, H. L. Mencken, George Jean Nathan and any number of others in different creative bailiwicks.

I suggest that the only sound solution, where esthetic standards vary so militantly, is not fewer but more diverse critics of John Canaday's courage, perception, and subjective legerdemain.

GEORGE R. CLAY.

Princeton, N. J.

Having read the protest signed by Messrs. Ackerman through Weiss against Mr. Canaday's critical vocabulary, we should like to put in a few words in his support. Generalizations and polemics, whether they concern current or past traditions in art or literature (and we must admit to being more familiar with the latter category), have long had an established place in criticism, have, indeed, been practised by most great critics. Often, but not always, it has appeared that the more sweeping the generalization, the more forthright (or injurious) the language, the more effective the criticism. The bite, not the justice, of the commentary is often what makes it memorable, and perhaps in the long run more valuable.

Consider Ben Jonson's observations on Spenser and Donne, Dryden's attack on Shadwell ("For Writing Treason and for Writing dull"), Pope's broadsides against Theobald, Cibber and Addison ("A tim'rous foe, and a suspicious friend")—this is insulting language at its best. Dryden and Pope were not just attacking their subjects' professional competence; like many critics, they were wreaking a personal vengeance by slandering their motives as well, and very effective—judged by its longevity—this kind of thing is. Sam Johnson wrote most unfair and injurious essays about Cowley and the Metaphysical poets; T. S. Eliot abused Milton and Edmund Wilson is most effectively unjust to the detective story. The value of these essays lies in the response which they provoked, and herein lies the ultimate value of good, if obstreperous criticism: its readers react strongly; they re-examine and re-evaluate the texts, canvases, and movements under attack.

The list of eminent critics who have recognized the value of what Messrs. Ackerman through Weiss term "insulting" critical language could be extended indefinitely: there is Goldsmith's superb excoriation of sentimental comedy; there is Ruskin's immortal comment on Whistler's "Nocturne," and Ruskin's critics savagely attacking him; there are the writings of T. E. Hulme, Irving Babbitt, H. L. Mencken and others. These critics certainly were not fair; many of them were not even right. On the other hand, many critics have been most eminently fair and extremely dull. Their writings had little or no effect upon their time; cautious and correct though they may have been, they are not remembered today.

We remember with delight Mr. Canaday's first appearance in the Sunday Times not so very long ago. That column, "Happy New Year," dealing with the estate of modern art, was read aloud by one of our family to the exultant delight of all who heard it. Here was a critic with something to say and a positive manner of saying it; here was a man saying what needed to be said in a respected journal of wide circulation. Mr. Canaday may often have been wrong—we do not have enough knowledge about contemporary works of art to evaluate even the majority of his opinions—but as works of criticism, his articles have never disappointed us. There are so few outspoken critics writing for any publication today that it would be a shame to gag those we have.

It will be remembered that Whistler finally won his suit against the dynamic Ruskin who was forced to pay a farthing in damages. It may well be that Mr. Canaday owes a farthing here and there. But we wish him a long reign in the pages of The Times. His critics would reduce his columns to the toothless mediocrity characteristic of most reviewing today. No more can be said in his support.

PETER S. PRESCOTT.

New York. ANNE PRESCOTT.

It is not only permissible, but often necessary for the critic to be a crusader—which, after all, is just an agitator you happen to agree with. William Lloyd Garrison found slavery deeply entrenched in the laws and institutional life of America, and began his thirty years of attack by saying "I will *be as* harsh as truth, and as uncompromising as justice." He was for years accused of an unnecessary intemperance of language—but he has been vindicated by the judgment of history.

HOWARD N. MEYER.

Rockville Centre, N. Y.

A critic's function is to criticize, not merely applaud.

PAUL HOLLISTER JR.

New York.

I was shocked and outraged at the vulgar, vitriolic attack on Mr. Canaday. I would not have objected to reasonable criticism from the group, but I do object to the vicious and scurrilous temper of their letter. I object, on grounds of decency, to quoting Mr. Canaday out of context. I object to packing the list of signators with many names that have no business in the fields of either art or art criticism. The entrenched group that fostered this attack has had a long period in which they dominated the written pages of art discussion. They have their own magazine. They have had the support of the museums. Surely, if they were confident and secure, the appearance of Mr. Canaday's column would not stir them to hysteria.

HARRY STERNBERG.

Glen Cove, N. Y.

The issue is not so much "the freaks, charlatans and the misled who surround this handful of serious talented artists" but the incredible aesthetic tyranny which the signers as a group have imposed on American creative thought at home and abroad.

GEORGE SCHREIBER.

New York.

There have been, I believe, other efforts to silence John Canaday's voice, but heretofore they have failed.

There are, I have heard, strong forces of money and influence against him, as there would naturally be, but I believe John Canaday is the best and most outspoken art critic The Times has ever had.

EDWARD HOPPER.

New York.

Since Mr. Canaday has been condemned by so very powerful a group, I think it only appropriate that he be defended by completely powerless individuals. And it is certain that, thanks to that self-same group, there can be no individual in this country more powerless than a nonabstract painter.

The students in universities *are* brainwashed: ask any refugee from Yale. The Paris-New York dealer axis *is* run like something out of a René Clair film except that, if you take art seriously, it is a good deal less funny. And as for the "nature of abstract expressionism" allowing for "exceptional tolerance"—I think that each member of the protest group should be forced to publish a set of standards by which an art that rejects both craftsmanship and draftsmanship can be judged.

PETER TODD MITCHELL.

New York.

It comes as a shock that a supposedly intelligent and important critic could wilfully neglect and malign the most important art movement that this country has ever originated and participated in.

TONI WIEN.

New York.

It seems to me that Mr. Canaday's real strength as a critic lies not only in his prose style, but in his catholicity of taste, which is perhaps misinterpreted by a group which has become somewhat parochial in its outlook.

THOMAS BARTEK.

Seymour, Conn.

Only two names among the forty-nine signers to that attack on John Canaday surprise me. I would have thought that Stanley Kunitz and Willem de Kooning had enough intelligence and self-respect to steer clear of such an obvious cabal. Any honest observer whose senses have not been paralyzed by the verbal chicanery of Art News or by the Museum of Modern Art's capitulation to chic, will know that the signers are defending a point of view obsolete ten years ago. Their vested interest in that point of view is manifest in their pique and their readiness to tear Mr. Canaday's charges out of context.

I might add that I am in an excellent position to defend Mr. Canaday since he has made it very clear that he has as little use for the new humanists whose art I believe in as he has for the latter-day sleepwalkers.

SELDEN RODMAN.

Oakland, N. J.

I own, among others, works by Willem de Kooning, Adolph Gottlieb, David Hare and Raymond Parker, but I was appalled at the letter signed by these artists and other well-known artists, critics, scholars and collectors. The evidence they offer plainly shows that the letter dealt with a single school of contemporary art to which many of the signators are publicly committed. The arguments decrying Mr. Canaday as a sort of critical Jack-the-Ripper raise the question of whether the motive behind the attack was not really an attempt by an artistic power elite to dictate what should and should not be written about abstract expressionism.

(MRS.) IOLA S. HAVERSTICK.

Southport, Conn.

I believe that it is not only the duty of the critic to stimulate interest in constructive tendencies, but to expose fraud where he sees it. I wonder why the signers of this letter felt that the "terminology of insults" was directed at them?

DANIEL R. BUTTERLY.

Cambria Heights, N. Y.

Many of us have felt for a long time that Mr. Canaday does not have those qualities that are essential to a critic: honesty, integrity, freedom from malice and the ability to see. His presence on your staff is entirely incongruous with the general excellence and principle of The Times.

RICHARD STANKIEWICZ.

New York.

Many of us artists have lost faith in the competence and integrity of art magazines such as Art News. That which distinguishes John Canaday is an honest opinion. We artists can only look to newspapers for honest criticism. The art magazines are suspect.

KARL KNATHS.

Provincetown, Mass.

I am one of those who believe, like Yeats, that all art critics are a bunch of flies kicking around the marmalade; however, if one must have them, they should be articulate and courageous, and if I am right in that belief, Mr. Canaday is certainly one up on any of the signers of that letter, whether the signer be poet, critic or painter. I only wish that Mr. Canaday had chosen a less dubious profession.

W. LEE SAVAGE.

Piermont, N. Y.

It is incredulous (sic) and amazing Mr. Canaday's slanderous and maligning remarks have continued so long and have been permitted to continue in your newspaper. I can only ascribe this to an unfortunate lapse of responsibility on the part of the editors.

SHEPHERD SCHREIBER.

New York.

I want to congratulate The Times on having a man of the caliber of Mr. Canaday as art critic. To him art did not begin this morning nor will it end tomorrow. He knows the art of the past and is able to write clearly and critically of the present. He is an outspoken and healthy asset to the art world.

WILLIAM ZORACH.

New York.

Many of the signers of the letter about John Canaday were people deserving of great respect, and some of them are people I am fond of. Few of them, I think, would deny that there has been for some time a "new academy" or a new academism.

We need independent criticism.

WINSLOW AMES.

Saunderstown, R. I.

Hooray for the Canaday spanking. This poor man has trudged through so many galleries and has endured so much, I certainly feel he should merit a change of assignment. I would love to read excerpts in which he expresses enthusiasm for a current, unrecognized artist. Or is it possible there is no *new* talent painting today that deserves recognition?

WILLIAM L. EASTON.

New York.

Mr. Canaday must expect that if he uses the pages of The New York Times to insinuate that artists are animated primarily by a wish to earn a quick dollar or by a devilish desire to fool the public, the artists and many of his readers in turn might begin to suspect that he is pandering to the prejudices of the street in the hope of selling more papers.

MILLARD MEISS.

Princeton, N. J.

Does not all this smell of the put-up job, the concerted effort of a bigoted group to silence a voice capable on occasion of opposing their point of view? There is no question whatever of *which* point of view is to be defended. This effort to suppress freedom of expression must be censured by anyone who regards freedom of the press as an essential liberty.

JOHN KOCH.

New York.

Mr. Canaday has elevated his profession from the level of press agentry and lobbying in the service of pressure groups to the status of truly independent art criticism.

HANS SAHL.

New York.

On numerous occasions Mr. Canaday has overstepped the bounds of art criticism and has used the pages of The New York Times for personal outbursts beyond the limits of decent criticism. I am constantly astonished that the pages of your newspaper can be used for this type of journalism.

ROBERT C. SCULL.

Great Neck, N. Y.

I heartily agree that Mr. Canaday must not be interfered with in expressing his opinion unequivocally.

LEE GATCH AND ELSIE DRAKE.

Lambertville, N. J.

I think that Mr. Canaday should be listened to rather than quarreled with. And I think this about Mr. Hess [Editor of "Art News"], too.

ISABEL BISHOP.

New York.

Mr. Canaday once remarked in one of his columns that he was writing for the broad, untutored (in art) audience rather than for the few, the interested or the knowing. Then have him take the name of humorist, or columnist, or fiction writer, not critic. For the critic, whether he will have it so or not, assesses the art of others and makes the audience, perhaps less perceptive than he, aware of its value through his knowledge, his sensitivity and his *sympathy*.

HELENE MCKINSEY.

New York.

Mr. Canaday has contributed nothing to my art education but a great deal to worsening my digestive system.

ISRAEL ROSEN, M. D.

Baltimore.

Anyone who can make so many distinguished people so angry must be doing a good job.

KARL M. ELISH.

Middleburgh, N. Y.